MOTHER WARRIORS

MOTHER
WARRIORS

A Nation of Parents Healing
Autism Against All Odds

JENNY McCARTHY

DUTTON
Published by Penguin Group (USA) Inc.
375 Hudson Street, New York, New York 10014, U.S.A.
Penguin Group (Canada), 90 Eglinton Avenue East, Suite 700, Toronto, Ontario M4P 2Y3, Canada (a division of Pearson Penguin Canada Inc.); Penguin Books Ltd, 80 Strand, London WC2R 0RL, England; Penguin Ireland, 25 St Stephen's Green, Dublin 2, Ireland (a division of Penguin Books Ltd); Penguin Group (Australia), 250 Camberwell Road, Camberwell, Victoria 3124, Australia (a division of Pearson Australia Group Pty Ltd); Penguin Books India Pvt Ltd, 11 Community Centre, Panchsheel Park, New Delhi - 110 017, India; Penguin Group (NZ), 67 Apollo Drive, Rosedale, North Shore 0632, New Zealand (a division of Pearson New Zealand Ltd); Penguin Books (South Africa) (Pty) Ltd, 24 Sturdee Avenue, Rosebank, Johannesburg 2196, South Africa

Penguin Books Ltd, Registered Offices: 80 Strand, London WC2R 0RL, England

Published by Dutton, a member of Penguin Group (USA) Inc.

First printing, September 2008
10 9 8 7 6 5 4 3 2 1

Grateful acknowledgment for permission to reprint the story on pp. 106–8: "Welcome to Holland." Copyright © 1987 by Emily Perl Kingsley. All rights reserved. Reprinted by permission of the author.

 REGISTERED TRADEMARK—MARCA REGISTRADA

LIBRARY OF CONGRESS CATALOGING-IN-PUBLICATION DATA
McCarthy, Jenny, 1972–
Mother warriors : a nation of parents healing autism against all odds / by Jenny McCarthy.
p. cm.
ISBN 978-0-525-95069-1 (hardcover)
1. Parents of autistic children—United States—Biography. I. Title.
RJ506.A9M4254 2008
618.92'8588200922—dc22
                    2008024743

Printed in the United States of America
Set in Granjon
Designed by Katy Riegel

To all the warriors who have come before me and to all the warriors who
will come after. Just know that even
though they might have silenced some
of our children, they will never silence
us. Our voices will shake the ground
of those who were responsible until
all of our children are safe from harm.

Contents

Contents

Contents

Foreword

JENNY WARNED ME. She told me that her book was just "a little critical" of the American Academy of Pediatrics, the "club" I have belonged to my entire career. The AAP and the Centers for Disease Control and Prevention (CDC) are filled with doctors who not only don't believe the ideas in this book but actively ridicule them and spend a lot of money trying to disprove the causes and treatments so well presented when Jenny McCarthy and others in the cure-autism community speak and write.

I have read a lot of books about parents of children with autism and I've long wanted to write a simple book about causes and treatments. This book is *much* more than that. The concepts are best articulated by Francis Collins's quote "Genetics loads the gun and environment pulls the trigger," and the notion that nobody knows your child better than you do.

Vaccines can *cause* autism.

Diet and supplements and other alternatives to doing nothing can lead to *recovery* from autism. Period.

We doctors need to stop deceiving our patients into thinking that immunizations are "free." Every medical intervention costs the body something, and we have a legal and moral obligation to tell parents.

When I give, for example, amoxicillin for a urinary tract infection, I'm almost apologetic as I describe the rash the kids can get, the possible yeast infections, and the diarrhea that can be caused by this and most other antibiotics. One in ten thousand children could have a dangerous allergic reaction.

When I discuss vaccines with parents, I talk to them about the benefits and the risks. The official position of the American Academy of Pediatrics may be the same as my personal position, but they are far too involved with the pharmaceutical industry to actually do anything but pay lip service to an open discussion. The CDC and the AAP are filled with doctors whose research, speaking engagements, and travel are often funded by the manufacturers of vaccines. Many of these same doctors are paid consultants, and some later go to work full-time for the pharmaceutical industry. They have called Jenny McCarthy and me "dangerous" for alerting parents to the possible risks of vaccinations. They forget that it was one of their own, Dr. Neal Halsey, who wrote the definitive article for the *Journal of the American Medical Association* in 1999. Entitled "Limiting Infant Exposure to Thimerosal in Vaccines and Other Sources of Mercury," this was the catalyst for removing most mercury from most vaccines. Dr. Halsey is a Professor of International Health and Pediatrics at Johns Hopkins University and he served on the Advisory Committee for Immunization Practices for the CDC and the Committee on Infectious Diseases of the AAP. He has never been anything but a strong advocate for vaccinations and adherence to the AAP's and CDC's immunization protocols.

The Summer 1999 issue of Hepatitis Control Report, featuring Dr. Halsey's findings and opinions, stated that "pediatricians who continue to administer thimerosal containing vaccines could face a flurry of lawsuits, perhaps claiming that children had acquired learning disabilities from mercury exposure." He didn't know just how prescient this statement was: I am writing this foreword some weeks after the U.S. Court of Federal Claims, which handles compensation to those people who claim injury from vaccines (dubbed the "vaccine court" by the press), issued an award to a family whose daughter developed autism after a series of vaccines. And, just this week, that same court is considering the cases of nearly five thousand other families whose children developed autism after vaccination.

Yes, most vaccines have much less mercury, but wait until the evidence against *aluminum* in vaccines becomes common knowledge. The body of research regarding aluminum's harm to human cells already contains hundreds of articles. The most damning conclusions were recently published by Dr. Robert Sears, a very well-known and well-respected pediatrician and the son and partner of Dr. William Sears, long regarded as "America's Pediatrician." Using the numbers he gathered from the Federal Drug Administration's (FDA) own data and Web site, Dr. Sears points out the unbelievable difference between the acknowledged toxic dose for a baby, 20 micrograms, and the amount found in the hepatitis B vaccine given on the day of birth, *250* micrograms. At two months of age, this same infant could receive immunizations containing as much as *1,875* micrograms of aluminum. This is disgraceful and dangerous, and Dr. Sears goes on to say that his "instinct was to assume that the issue had been properly researched, and that studies had been done on healthy infants to determine their ability to rapidly excrete aluminum."

No studies have been done. None. He, and we, can conclude what scientists have known for a long time: Evidence has existed for years that aluminum in amounts this large is harmful to humans. We can only guess what harm we might be causing to *babies* with these huge overdoses of aluminum.

In mid-2008, Dr. Bernadine Healy finally spoke up. Dr. Healy is the former head of the United States National Institutes of Health (NIH) and a key member of the Institute of Medicine. Referring to the association between thimerosal, vaccines, and autism, Dr. Healy said, "I think public health officials have been too quick to dismiss the hypothesis as 'irrational,' without sufficient studies of causation... without studying the population that got sick." I believe she's just one of many intelligent doctors and scientists who know that we need to study the link between vaccines and autism and other neuroimmune disorders.

Like many of you and like some of my colleagues, I'm extremely concerned about what has caused the tremendous increase in autism and related disorders over the past decade. The presumption that doctors are much better at diagnosis is absurd and unscientific. (I know that I'm not 400 or 800 percent smarter than I was years ago.) The truth is that we have to look much harder at what happens when we directly and repeatedly inject toxic material into babies, toddlers, and children. The benefits for most healthy children are easily matched or outweighed by the risks of the immunization schedule used by almost all pediatricians. Some of our vaccines have outlived their usefulness in the United Sates and elsewhere, and others need reformulation to make them safer for those families who want their children to receive them. Additionally, pediatricians and the medical community at large have to begin listening very closely to parents who know their children better than we do.

Last but far from least, we have to support and reinforce the intelligent and fiercely held *hope* these parents of children with autism have. Doctors have to acknowledge and help research the therapies that lead to recovery from autism, recovery brought on by therapies long ignored by the AAP and others. Dairy-free, gluten-free, sugar-free diets have succeeded far too many times for any doctor to claim that they're not "evidence-based." Evidence doesn't spring just from medical studies funded by drug companies and supervised by MDs and researchers on their payrolls. Evidence can come from the hundreds of families and doctors who have watched children with autism get better and even fully recover from the symptoms that have kept them from main-stream education and social opportunities. This is hard evidence and to deny it is specious reasoning and bad science. Behavioral therapy works; hyperbaric oxygen works; evaluation and treatment of intestinal infection can lead to lessening of symptoms and a dramatic improvement in the quality of life for these children and their families.

Medical interventions have caused many cases of autism. Jenny McCarthy presents a case for medical interventions that can lead to recovery. This book is meant to be read *not* with sadness but rather with lots of hope for the future.

Jay N. Gordon, M.D., F.A.A.P., I.B.C.L.C., F.A.B.M.
Assistant Clinical Professor of Pediatrics,
UCLA Medical Center
Former Senior Fellow in Pediatric Nutrition,
Memorial Sloan-Kettering Institute

PART ONE

The Time Is Now

1

Opening the Can of Worms

I TOOK A STEP toward my chair and then stopped quickly. Suddenly I couldn't put one foot in front of the other. I looked down at the pretty powder-blue dress that I'd bought months ago and I couldn't help notice that the hem was shaking. My knees were clicking against each other like a little girl about to say something to the class for the very first time. As people moved quickly around me, I stayed in this moment paralyzed by the events that were about to unfold. I closed my eyes to gather strength. How did I get here? Why me? It would have been so much easier to stay quiet and blend in with the rest of the world without anyone knowing my pain. I'm so scared. I'm so scared. I'm so scared.

"Jenny," the stagehand said. "We're going live in five minutes. You need to sit down."

I looked down in front of me and prayed to God to give me strength. I opened my heart and then looked back at the stagehand. He put his hand on my shoulder and said, "Oprah will be out there in a minute."

My eyes welled up as I slowly began walking. I exited the dark room in which I had waited, shaking and praying, and soon entered the studio, bright with lights and filled with women. I faintly heard the sound of applause, but the tone of the applause was different from what I was used to hearing. It wasn't a frantic slapping of hands with big grins on everyone's faces. It was slow, deep, and sympathetic. I sat down in my seat and looked at the crowd. I witnessed a room filled with five hundred women who had now grown silent. They looked at me encouragingly and I took a few deep breaths to center myself.

Then the room ignited with applause, the type of applause that is excited and brings people to their feet. Oprah had just stepped onto the stage and began walking toward me. The energy in the room was electric. She calmly waved to her fans, who I'm sure had waited years to see her, and I could tell from the looks on their faces that it was already worth the long wait. She arrived in front of me and I stood up to hug her. On any other day I would have gotten on my knees and kissed her toenails, but today was too important for worship. She knew it and I knew it.

We sat down and the stagehand said, "Two minutes till live."

Oprah beamed and said, "I love live!" and the audience chuckled.

As she gathered her notes, I leaned over and softly said to her, "My intention today is to offer hope, faith, recovery."

She smiled and responded, "Well, then let us say it again. The intention for the show today is hope, faith, and recovery." From her energy at that moment, I had no doubt she was right.

"We are LIVE in...FIVE, FOUR, THREE, TWO, ONE."

Oprah's voice echoed in the theatre, "If your child stopped speaking, wouldn't look you in the eye, and completely ignored the world around them, what would you do?"

Being trained in the world of show business, I knew I had only seven minutes in this first segment to tell my story. I kept telling myself, "Don't cry, don't cry. Tell your story, Jenny." I took a deep breath and began to speak publicly for the first time about the horrific events that had taken place in the past two years.

IT BEGAN ONE MORNING in 2005. I had awakened with an uncomfortable feeling, like something was wrong. I noticed the clock showed 7:45. I thought it was unusual because Evan always got up at 7:00 A.M. on the dot every morning. My motherly instinct started screaming at me to run to his nursery. I opened the door and ran to his crib and found him convulsing and struggling to breathe. His eyes were rolled back in his head. I picked him up and started screaming at the top of my lungs. The paramedics finally arrived and it took about twenty minutes to get Evan's body to stop convulsing.

When we finally arrived at the hospital, the doctors told

me that he had a febrile seizure, caused by a fever. I told the doctor, "You know, he doesn't really have a fever, so how does that play in the scenario?"

The doctor responded by saying, "Well, he could have been getting one."

That didn't make sense to me at all. I went home with my baby, thinking something was very wrong. I didn't know what it was, but everything inside of me was screaming that there had to be something more.

About three weeks after the initial seizure, Evan had a second episode. We were visiting Evan's grandparents when I noticed a kind of stoned look on his face. I passed him off to Grandma thinking he was just tired, but moments later his eyes rolled into the back of his head and I knew it was happening again. I frantically called 911 and put cold rags on him (which is what you do for febrile seizures). This seizure was different, though. His body wasn't convulsing this time, nor was he trying to breathe. Foam was coming out of his mouth and he began to turn pale. I put my hand on his chest and kept saying, "Stay with me, baby, stay with me."

Then the worst of the worst happened. I felt his heart stop. I fell to my knees as I watched Evan's eyes dilate and watched his lifeless body lay still. The paramedics rushed in and began to perform CPR on him. All I could do in my head was scream, "Why? Why? Why?" Then I heard a voice inside of me say, "Everything is going to be okay." I didn't know how I was able to stay calm in the midst of the hell we were in, but peace had suddenly come over my whole body.

After two minutes, the paramedics revived Evan. I silently screamed, "Thank you, God. Thank you, God."

Because there were no helicopters available, we had to transport Evan to the Los Angeles hospital by ambulance. It was a three-hour car ride and in that time he had another seizure. At the hospital he had seven more seizures within a seven-hour period and after two days of being there and wondering what was going on, they came to me with the diagnosis of epilepsy. My instinct was screaming, "There's more, there's more!" I decided to get a second opinion and met with one of the best neurologists in the world. He politely put his hand on me and said, "I'm sorry, your son has autism."

I died in that moment but my instincts told me that this man was right. All those beautiful characteristics that I thought were Evan—the hand flapping, the toe walking, the playing with door hinges and lining up toys—weren't Evan characteristics at all. Who was my son if he wasn't all these things? The neurologist saw the look on my face and said to me, "Hey, this is the same little boy you came in this room with. He's not any different. He's the same boy." I looked at the doctor and replied, "No, he's not. My son is trapped inside this label called autism and I'm gonna get him out."

WHEN I FINISHED TELLING the story of my ordeal with Evan, Oprah smiled proudly and uttered, "We'll be right back."

I took a big deep breath and leaned back in my chair, though I knew the hard part was not over. I knew at home millions of mothers had been waiting years for what was coming in the segment after the commercial break. Mothers who have been silenced, mothers whose child's own pediatrician had called them stupid and ignorant, mothers who had been accused of causing their child's autism with their own negligence, mothers who had waited years for one person to break through in the media and say what they have been screaming for a whole decade. This wasn't my moment in the spotlight coming up. It was theirs. I was their voice and ready to speak on behalf of these amazing women.

"FIVE, FOUR, THREE, TWO, ONE."

When the red light on the camera came on and we were back on the air, Oprah asked me to explain why I think Evan became autistic. In that next moment I actually smiled. At first I couldn't believe I was smiling and I imagined watching that moment on TiVo, screaming at myself again and again, "Why are you smiling?" And then it clicked. Oprah was finally giving me the chance to speak about Evan's autism without being censored. That's why I cracked a smile: The truth was about to come out of my mouth.

"The statistics are one in one-fifty. I'd like to know what number will it take, what number does it have to be for everyone to start listening to what the mothers of children who have autism have been saying for years, which is... We vaccinated our baby and SOMETHING happened. SOMETHING happened. Why won't anyone believe us?"

The audience began to clap that deep, sympathetic applause again. I looked around and saw tears on the faces of mothers who I knew had children affected with autism. It seemed as though their anger had been released in that brief moment.

I continued to speak about how the Centers for Disease Control (CDC) acts as if vaccines are one-size-fits-all, as if they should be administered at the same rate for all children without regard to the individual child's needs and biological makeup, and I felt something even more profound. I felt the collective energy of all moms everywhere. I felt them jumping up and down on their couches, I felt them glued to their TV screens, crying and raising up their arms, I felt them calling their own moms on the phone screaming, "Are you hearing this?! She said it!"

Oprah finished with a statement from the CDC, which said there was no science to support the connection between vaccines and autism. I couldn't help but think, "Who needs science when I'm witnessing it every day in my own home? I watched it happen." I replied with all the love that I could muster in my heart. "At home, Evan is my science."

Oprah smiled warmly into the camera and then again cut to a commercial. As soon as I saw the red light on the camera go off, I leaped out of my chair and walked offstage to relax my pent-up nerves. I had just opened a giant can of worms and I wasn't sure what the reaction would be. I tossed my concerns aside and centered myself. Today was the first day that anyone was allowed to speak freely about vaccines, and Oprah was the first to allow it. It might have been news to some people, but mothers who have children on the autism spectrum know. People we told about the vaccine connection called us crazy and desperate to blame, but we've lived with our children and have watched them suffer. I could understand if only a few mothers were speaking out, but when millions of mothers are screaming that something happened when their child was vaccinated, I think it's time the world listened to what we have to say.

I sat back down and looked at Oprah. She smiled at me and I knew I had made her proud for speaking from my heart. I was excited about the upcoming segment because I was going to talk about recovery. I knew many people watching didn't know that children with autism can recover from it. Even people who have children with autism knew of no such thing. The hard part for me was knowing that the treatments I was about to discuss would cost people more money because insurance doesn't cover treatments for autism. But I had to say it. People needed to know this information, and pediatricians aren't offering it.

I explained to Oprah that with the proper diet, kids were getting better. I talked about the gut-brain connection: "Cleaning up the gut clears the brain. The connection is very real," I said.

A doctor once said to me that if people don't believe in the gut-brain connection, then tell them to go try that theory in a bar. Order a drink and see what happens. I witnessed with my own son how food alters brain response. Within two weeks of starting the diet, Evan doubled his vocabulary and the foggy world he seemed to be trapped in suddenly lifted.

Oprah said I was going to hear a lot of backlash from people for whom the diet didn't or wouldn't work. I wanted to say, "Yes, I know and it hurts my heart on a level that no one could possibly understand. I walked in these moms' shoes. I know what it feels like to hope for a miracle, and it haunts me to this day knowing that for many, it wouldn't do anything except empty pockets. But I know for MANY children it will work. For the kids who are able to speak for the first time or smile for the first time because of the information I just shared with their parents, it was worth it." But my segment was coming to an end so I had to make a point quickly.

"I'm just a mom telling a story that resembles many other moms' stories. Our kids *do* get better. It's like chemotherapy. It doesn't work for every cancer victim, but you're gonna give it a try."

Oprah replied, "Yes I am."

As Oprah went to a commercial break I knew my work here was coming to a close. I shut my eyes and asked God if there was anything I needed to squeeze in because the last segment was coming up. I sat in silence for a moment as Oprah talked to Holly Robinson Peete. Then it hit me....

TWO MONTHS PRIOR

Sitting in my house while on the phone doing my preinterview for *20/20* I had what most people would call a breakdown. My boyfriend, Jim, called it a breakthrough, but the breakdown had to happen first.

I hung up the phone with the *20/20* producers and put my hand over my heart. It was beating fast, as though I had just run a marathon. I wasn't nervous about the interview and I didn't feel stressed out, so I couldn't understand where these heart palpitations were coming from. I stepped outside and took a few deep breaths, but it didn't help.

That night I decided to sleep in Evan's room with him. I thought that I might be sensing an upcoming seizure, as I had in the past. As I lay glued to him with my eyes wide open, the feeling in my chest got worse. I started to sweat and then I began to panic that something was terribly wrong with me. I ran to my good ol' computer and went to my favorite university: the University of Google. I searched for heart palpitations and it brought up anxiety and panic attacks. I sat back in my chair and realized that Google was right. I wasn't dying of a heart attack; I was simply having a panic attack. I couldn't believe that I had gone through the past two years—dealing with the emotional roller coaster of autism, watching Evan have seizures, and even watching him go into cardiac arrest—without ever having a panic attack. Why NOW when everything seemed okay?

I was just about to publish my book *Louder Than Words*, and I wondered if, on a subconscious level, I was scared out of my mind about telling the world for the first time about my experiences with Evan. I didn't think that was it, though. Don't get me wrong, I was scared but this was not the reason for my panic attacks. I went down the list of possible worries: Evan's health, my debt, my relationship. They all came back negative. Nothing resonated.

WHY WHY WHY? I wondered. I decided to do the actress thing and take a pill to go to sleep that night. I still lay glued to Evan on the off chance that my mommy seizure radar was the cause of my anxiety.

The next morning I woke up and looked at Evan sleeping sideways on the bed. His cute cheeks were smashed on my chest and he was looking up at me. He blinked his big blue eyes and said, "It's going to be a beautiful day."

I smiled back at him and said, "Yes, it is, Evan...a BEAUTIFUL day." I gave thanks for the words that came out of his mouth and then tickled him to tears. After I released him from the tickle machine, he ran to go play and my panic attack returned with a vengeance. "What the hell?" I thought.

I called Jim at his house. "Something is up and I can't get a grip. I can hardly breathe."

"What's bothering you?" he asked, and I said, "Nothing." He then told me to call my therapist. She was the woman who convinced me to get a divorce and I hadn't talked to her in two years. But I hung up from Jim and took his advice.

My therapist answered the phone and I explained to her what was going on. She paused for a moment and then said, "You have never dealt with the fact that you feel guilty for Evan's autism."

I was silent for a moment and then replied, "No, Evan's pediatrician is guilty for his autism."

She said, "You need to get in here. You have never dealt with this. It's always been about your ex or money or autism in general but never your guilt."

I didn't want to hear this. I wanted to get off the phone with her, so I quickly replied, "Okay, I'll call you next week to set something up." I hung up and sank into my chair completely stumped.

That night I decided to sleep at Jim's house, hoping he could offer some relief. My fast-beating heart and I walked in the door and he gave me a big kiss, the kind of kiss that says "everything's gonna be okay, baby." We went into the kitchen and I sat my butt up on the kitchen counter. We talked for a little bit and then he asked, "So, what did your therapist say?"

I stopped for a moment to giggle in my head. Growing up in the Midwest, I used to think only crazy people saw therapists and even though I've been in Hollywood for fourteen years, having a therapist still makes me laugh. I replied nonchalantly, "She said that I feel guilty for Evan's autism."

Jim stopped what he was doing and slowly looked at me. He stared at me and in that moment I felt naked. I looked into his eyes and saw for the first time that I had built these thick walls of defense around my heart. I knew love was capable of a lot, but I had no idea that the man standing in front of me would be the one to put the first crack in those walls. He softly said with the sweetest eyes, "You do feel guilty for Evan's autism."

He slowly walked over to me and held me. I know it might be confusing that any mom could feel guilty for her child's autism, but some do. Some moms feel that it must have been something in them that caused their perfect babies to be born with weak immune systems. Some moms worry that they didn't scream loudly enough when they had concerns about the vaccinations.

I gripped the back of Jim's shirt and put my head in his neck and cried hard. I cried for my guilt. I cried out to Evan for letting him down. I told him I was sorry I didn't protect him. I cried for his physical pain. I cried for the seizure that caused him to go into cardiac arrest. I cried for being so alone in my pain. I cried for my fear. I cried for not feeling safe anymore. I cried for every mom in the world who was going through what I had gone through.

Two hours had gone by and I slowly lifted my head. I felt a sense of peace, but I also felt incredibly vulnerable and stupid for crying so hard. I always wanted to at least appear that I had all my shit together, that I was a strong woman who could handle anything that came my way, including autism. I wasn't sure Jim would admire this new girl who had just shown her bloody wounds. But when I told him how naked I felt, he told me, "I never loved you as much as I do in this moment. Right now." He told me to keep crying as things come up, and to my surprise, they kept coming up. The next morning I lay in bed and cried more, and this continued for at least four days. I felt stupid at times, but I couldn't keep it buried any longer. The well had opened and I had to release the emotion, any time and any place. I'd even cry my ass off on the side of the road.

I realized that when Evan was diagnosed I hadn't allowed myself to grieve. I cried but I didn't grieve the fear, guilt, anger, and resentment I had in me. I said to myself back then, "There is no time for me or my feelings. I need to focus on getting Evan better and that's that." Now that Evan was better, I realized I had never gone back to deal with my own pain over the diagnosis.

When the doctor first gave me Evan's diagnosis, I popped a Valium as soon as we got to the car. Drugs and alcohol take the pain away, but eventually the effect of the drugs wears off and the pain comes back. It's easy to become addicted to the drugs as the pain becomes more and more unbearable, but instead of turning to drugs I simply suppressed my pain. I was amazed that I had been completely unaware that this deep-rooted guilt existed in me. I believe that suppressed emotion causes disease, so the faster you start to FEEL, the faster you can HEAL. Sitting behind the wheel at a red light, crying my eyes out, I knew Mommy's healing had begun.

I LOOKED UP and saw Oprah staring at me. "Go ahead, Jenny. You wanted to say something. You get the last word."

I looked out at the cameras and all the eager moms in the audience and realized it was the last segment. This was it. I said, "Don't feel guilty for your child's autism. It's not your fault. Stay focused on recovery and trust your instincts."

Oprah smiled and said, "And ONE SIZE DOES NOT FIT ALL!"

I wanted to leap over that chair and give her a big fat kiss, but I knew I'd probably never be asked to come back to the show, so I simply replied, "Yes, one size does not fit all."

The stagehand shouted, "We're out." The camera lights went dark and everyone started to get up.

I walked over to Oprah and said, "Thank you on behalf of thousands of moms for allowing me to speak our truth." She gave me a hug that was filled with love, warmth, and gratitude. I didn't have to tell her how profound this show was. She felt it. I walked back to my dressing room relieved and said a little prayer that my intention to offer hope, faith, and recovery for these families was successful.

LATER THAT NIGHT I sat down at my computer to answer e-mails from viewers on oprah.com, as Oprah had promised on the show. Every time I tried signing on, it would sign me off or say "incorrect password." I was so frustrated. I pictured these moms frantically writing and waiting for me to respond, and it was killing me not to be able to answer them.

Finally I called my segment producer on her cell phone, and she said, "The system crashed. After the show, there were 2,500 hits per second and it completely crashed the entire system." In a way, I wasn't at all surprised. I knew the show would have such an amazing impact, since no one until this point had spoken about vaccines and, more important, recovery! I had also talked about how the gluten-free, casein-free diet was helping kids with autism, a theory that has always been controversial. It would surely stir up some shit, and I was interested to see what people would be saying about the diet. I wanted to know if others across the country had tried it or any other therapies that might have led to their kids getting better.

Two days later oprah.com was working and I could finally read some of the e-mails that had been posted. Mom after mom reported similar improvements after changing their child's diet and trying other biomedical treatments like oxygen therapy and metals detoxification. I was so happy that the rest of the world would see now that Evan is not alone. Healing is a possibility for every child with autism. Hope, faith, recovery. What an awesome intention!

IT HAD BEEN A WEEK since I was on Oprah, and I still wasn't sure what the reaction of the country was going to be. I walked around looking over my shoulder, waiting for people to either hug me or throw something at me. I was also a little bit scared about pharmaceutical companies. If my life were a movie, the Centers for Disease Control and the pharmaceutical companies would all be having secret meetings plotting to discredit or quiet me.

On my way to New York City to continue my press tour for *Louder Than Words*, I was really nervous. I knew Oprah was open-minded and understanding of everything I had to say, but I had a strange instinctual feeling that someone along this path was going to challenge me. I knew during the tour that the pain I had gone through with Evan's brave struggle would sometimes be overshadowed by the controversy of autism, but it was important to get the message out on a massive scale. I kept my heart open and knew that whatever happened would be for the best reason possible. But I had already experienced so much pain and I was hoping I wouldn't have to go through any more pain just for speaking the truth. I was about to find out that there were many moms like me who were made to feel stupid for speaking this truth, and I was going to be the one to knock down some walls.

2

Imagine

IMAGINE WATCHING YOUR CHILD climb up a flight of stairs. He slips on a stair and cuts his knee open and begins gushing blood. The cuts are deep, and you immediately wash away the blood, wrap up the knee, and head to the hospital. Once you get there, the doctor asks what happened. You reply, "He climbed up some stairs and he fell and got hurt."

Now imagine the doctor telling you it's not possible that your child got this hurt from stairs. "But I saw him climb stairs and fall and I saw his knee split open," you explain.

Again, the doctor says, "It's not possible."

And you repeat, "But I saw it happen!"

Then the doctor tells you that climbing up stairs is safe. But you know what you saw with your own eyes and so you insist, "But obviously sometimes it's NOT safe. Look at my child. I saw him get hurt!"

The doctor just keeps shaking his head and denies that stairs could ever harm a child.

This is how black and white it is for us moms who have children with autism. We had healthy beautiful children who climbed up stairs perfectly until one stair caused them to fall. We have witnessed the neurological downfall of our children after certain vaccinations, but when we tell the doctors what we saw, they don't believe us. Can you imagine how frustrating this is?

Let's take the stair scenario a step further. After the doctor rejects your claims, you decide to treat the wound yourself. You learn about natural and alternative treatments, which you try out, and your child's knee heals to the point where you can barely see any marks. Now imagine you go to the doctor for a follow-up visit and this time you see a different doctor. The doctor looks at your child's knee strangely and says, "This must be the wrong knee."

You explain, "No, this is the knee that split open."

The doctor says, "It can't be because it healed up. There is no way an injury like that could heal. The hospital must have mistaken the severity of the wound."

You reply, "No, doctor, I healed the wound myself by cleaning it out and treating my child with natural remedies."

The doctor then looks at you strangely. He begins to laugh at you and tells you that your son never really had an open wound to begin with. You stand there with your mouth open.

"Yes, he did, doctor. Take a look at the medical records. He was seen in YOUR hospital!"

The doctor replies, "It must have been a mistake on his records. He never had a wound here."

This is exactly how it is when a child with autism gets better. No one believes he had anything wrong with him to begin with. People think these recovered children were misdiagnosed. The reason recovery is controversial is because we are healing these kids by treating the injuries caused by the vaccines or the environmental toxins rather than the autism itself. When we treat these things, the symptoms of the autism get better. The medical community is terrified to come within ten feet of detoxing metals out of these kids because it will point the finger directly at what everyone is so scared to admit. Vaccines CAN trigger autism.

There are two controversies about autism: first, the causes, and second, whether children can recover. A battle is raging in the medical community, but there is a growing army of mothers who are fighting for their children and witnessing recovery firsthand. Imagine a world in which we all are fighting on the same side to help make children with autism better. The time to unite is now.

3

"I'm Not Crazy!"

WHEN I FIRST FOUND OUT about the diet and supplements that were helping kids with autism, I kept saying, "Why isn't this on *20/20*? Why don't people know about it?" During the press tour for *Louder Than Words*, I was invited onto *20/20* to discuss just that. I'm so glad that *20/20* had the courage to talk about it. I asked God during the tour to send me only reporters who could help me get the message out clearly, and having Deborah Roberts as my on-camera interviewer was truly a blessing. It turns out that even though her son was not diagnosed with autism, he had some developmental delays and she was interested in trying the diet. I pleaded with her to get on it because I knew the diet also helps children who are not on the autism spectrum.

During the interview I talked extensively about vaccines, but *20/20* didn't air any of it. People thought I had gotten cold feet, but I didn't. In fact, it was one of the best informational interviews I'd done about vaccines. They edited it to mainly focus on diet and kids getting better. How can I argue or be upset with that?

After the interview aired, Deborah Roberts called to tell me that she had started her child on the diet and that people around her saw improvements in her son. As it turned out, along this journey, many would be saying the same thing.

While walking in JFK airport, a woman ran up to me and started screaming, "Thank you! Thank you!" At first I didn't know what was going on. Throughout my career, men have shouted to me in airports, "Nice boobs!" but I've never had women shouting, "Thank you!" I think this moment truly defined a turning point in my fan demographic. I stopped and smiled at her before heading to my car. Her eyeballs were practically bulging out of her head and she looked at me as if she had just seen Santa Claus. While huffing and puffing, she said, "Thank you! Thank you because now people...now people don't think I'm crazy." She put her arms around me and held me in a bear hug. I could tell the people I was traveling with had no idea what she meant, but I did. I smiled and hugged her back and we stayed in this hug while people hustled around us.

Many moms like this woman say that their own mothers, mothers-in-law, and best friends think they are crazy for believing in the vaccine implications and that food supplements and detox played a huge role in healing their children. The fact that I had validated this woman's experience made her feel less alone in her truth. The irony is that people around ME didn't believe me until I was on Oprah; it wasn't until Oprah that my own truth was validated. I gently separated from her and said, "I understand completely."

She smiled back and shouted, "Don't ever stop," and then walked away.

As I got into the car, I contemplated how universally perfect everything was. I believe in manifestations, and I believe that the collective energy of all of the women who had been waiting for someone to speak for them had manifested me as the one to do it. Truth be told, it would have been a lot easier if it had happened to someone else. I could have stayed on course as a comedian and watched my kid beat up other kids at school or watched him play soccer. I'd never have to endure endless emergency rooms, or have therapist after therapist come into my home, or have to dig through poop samples and collect pee samples. But these moms needed someone with balls, someone who could actually get booked on a talk show, and more important, a mom who went through hell and back to save her kid.

As we pulled away from the curb, I looked at the sky and sent these moms a message from my heart: "I am here and will do the job I came here to do. I won't let you down. I will never shut up. I am here. I am here. I am here."

4

Diane Sawyer Rocks!

I SAT IN MY CHAIR on the set of *Good Morning America* with a belly full of butterflies. I had never been on this show before even though *Louder Than Words* was my fourth book. They were never really interested in anything I had to say in the past and I couldn't really blame them. Everything in my past now seemed pointless.

As I attempted to sit like a lady and not like a truck driver, I noticed my left boob was convulsing. My heart was beating so hard it was making my left boob bounce up and down. I looked up at the cameramen and producers on set to see if anyone was noticing my possessed left boob. No one seemed aware but I couldn't keep my eyes off of it. I closed my eyes and said a prayer that I was not going to have a heart attack on live TV.

I opened my eyes and saw Diane Sawyer walking toward me. I have always been a fan of hers and thought that if I was ever interviewed by Diane Sawyer I'd know that I had really made it. Now, here she was, about to interview me. I still don't consider myself to have made it big, but she knew I was delivering a powerful message and that the world was now ready to listen. I was honored, to say the least, to be interviewed by her.

Diane did an amazing job guiding me through the interview. Halfway through it, I noticed that her copy of my book was dog-eared, highlighted, and had sticky notes all over it. My book in her hands looked like it had been through hell and back and I never felt more proud. Diane Sawyer had actually read my story. Not only did she read it, she beat the hell out of it. Most people might think, "Well, of course she read it, she's interviewing you." But that is not always the case; in fact, most TV interviewers don't read the books by the authors they interview. Usually the producers read and then give summaries to the interviewer along with questions. But not Diane. She worked it and I was honored.

As we talked about how the medical community doesn't understand that children with autism are actually physically sick and how pediatricians across the country have no idea how to fix them, I started to realize that this was something I needed to pursue a little bit harder in the press. Almost every mom I know with a kid on the autism spectrum has gone to a pediatrician who has NO IDEA that certain symptoms exist in these kids. Children with autism often have leaky guts, dysregulated immune systems, inflammation, food allergies, eczema, constipation, fungal overgrowth, and viral, thyroid, and cholesterol issues. Pediatricians tell parents that we are overreacting, that all kids get constipated or that diarrhea is just part of autism. They tell us that yeast or candida isn't real. As I was talking to Diane, I decided I had to go kick some ass in the pediatrician world as soon as I left the show.

The interview was coming to an end and I had so much to be grateful for. I didn't have a heart attack on live TV, I was energized to lead the fight against pediatricians, and Diane Sawyer never saw my boob bouncing to the beat of my heart.

5

Stan the Man

STAN KURTZ IS A FATHER I met who had succeeded in recovering his son. You will get to know him later as the only warrior dad in the book. He had become a real expert in biomedicine and he blew me away. I decided to take him on the media tour with me in case I needed any facts at the last second, and I'm glad I did. He was my rock and backbone during one of the most draining weeks of my life.

After I finished my interview with Diane Sawyer, I got off the stage and said to Stan, "Who is in charge of teaching the pediatricians about HOW to heal these kids? I keep bitching on TV that no one is doing anything about these doctors and I realized I need to make it happen."

"The AAP, the American Academy of Pediatrics," he replied.

I paused. "Why don't I just call them personally and insist they sit down with our scientists and Defeat Autism Now! doctors who have learned how to heal these kids?"

Stan answered, "The American Academy of Pediatrics has never met with the DAN! doctors and scientists. Not once in twelve years."

"Why?" I asked. "That's honestly insane!"

He replied, "I don't know. If there was a small tribe in Africa that was healing cancer, you would think we would all run down there to find out what they're doing."

"Not in the United States," I said. "The medical community would discredit the information because disease is much more profitable." It sounds like political propaganda, but personally I believe it.

When we got back to the hotel room, I had to do six more hours of phone interviews. I was so exhausted that I started to lose my voice. In the seventh hour, I had to cancel my last interview because I was physically and emotionally drained. I crawled into the hotel bed and pulled the blankets over my head. I started shivering and wanted to hide from the world for at least a month.

KNOCK KNOCK KNOCK.

I was in a hotel room in New York—who would possibly be knocking on my door? I figured there probably weren't any Mormons around, and I couldn't imagine who else could be at the door. I wriggled out of my bed and opened the door and there was Stan holding his cell phone up to me. He said, "I got an executive at the American Academy of Pediatrics on the phone for you."

WHAT?!!!

I grabbed the phone out of his hands and pressed MUTE. "Whattaya mean?"

He said, "You told me to get someone on the phone, so I did."

"Well, what did you tell them?" I asked.

"I told them Jenny McCarthy is on a large media tour and wants to speak to someone before she continues."

"Holy shit, Stan, holy shit!" I screamed.

I looked in the mirror to fix myself, as if that would actually help. I put the phone next to my ear and trusted that God would put the best words possible into my mouth to help make a change in the history of medicine.

"Hi there, this is Jenny McCarthy," I said. The man on the other end of the phone introduced himself and apologized because he was about to board a plane for France. I told him how much I appreciated his taking my phone call.

He said, "What are you looking for?" I smiled for a moment and tried to stay in control. I had to censor myself and pace my response.

"I'm sure you know I've been on a press tour and I've been bitching and moaning that pediatricians across the country do not know how to heal many of the ailments associated with autism."

He was silent and then responded, "I've seen some interviews."

"I would love nothing more in the world than to have the American Academy of Pediatrics sit down at a think tank that's coming up in a few weeks. All the top doctors and scientists in the field of autism will be teaching other doctors how to heal kids with autism. They have been recovering and helping kids for the past twelve years and have research to prove it."

Silence again, then the reply, "Um...I'm not the person who would be able to organize that. I can put you in touch with the person who does that."

"Great," I said. "Give me his number." He rattled off a number and I thanked him again for taking the time to listen. I hung up and hugged Stan. "We're doing it! We're finally gonna start getting these kids the health care they deserve." I chugged a bottle of water and sat down and immediately dialed the number he'd given me.

A woman answered the phone and I asked for her boss. She asked me what my call was regarding and I said it was Jenny McCarthy wanting to speak to him because his boss referred me.

"Hold on a second," she said and placed me on hold. All I could do was picture this little assistant running into her boss's office freaking out about what to say to me. I was hoping he would immediately pick up the phone and talk to me like a man, but no such luck. She came back and said, "Can you please be more specific?"

"Well," I responded, "I can be more specific on *The View* tomorrow morning or I can be more specific when he picks up the phone to talk to me."

"Can we call you back in a few minutes?"

"Sure," I replied and I gave her my cell phone number. I hung up and sat back in my chair. Sometimes when I want someone to do something they don't want to do, I pray to that person's guardian angel to help push them a little. So after I hung up the phone, I prayed that this guy's guardian angel would smack him in the head and say, "WAKE UP! Someone is trying to help out, man!"

RING RING RING.

Wow! Guardian angels rock! I picked up the phone.

"Hello?"

"Hi, we're calling for Jenny McCarthy."

"This is she," I replied.

"Hi, this is public relations at the American Academy of Pediatrics."

My jaw dropped. I couldn't believe they handed me off to the division that handles press for the organization. I said, "Why didn't he call me back? Why did he send you to me?"

"We need to know what the problem is," she responded.

Oh my God, did she just ask me what the "problem" is? Wow, was she about to get an earful....

"I'll tell you what the problem is. The problem is that one in ninety-four boys has autism and most of them have chronic illnesses such as leaky gut, candida, constipation, metals toxicity, viral infections, PANDAS, bad bacteria and measles stuck in the gut, inflammation of the brain, and almost every pediatrician in this country does not know how to treat these kids or even know these symptoms are associated with autism because the American Academy of Pediatrics does not have anything in their medical journal or whatever it is that teaches doctors how to treat the children. All they're doing is telling these moms that gut issues are not related and that candida is not real when we are watching yeast drip out of our kids' butts!"

Once again there was silence on the phone. "Well," she responded. "We are deeply involved with new treatment for autism. In fact in a couple of months we are coming out with a new protocol that requires pediatricians to screen for autism twice before the age of two."

"Listen, these kids are sick now, physically, do you hear me? That's great and all, but your doctors don't know how to treat these kids and they can learn if they just talk to the DAN! doctors, many of whom are pediatricians from the AAP. Cuz right now, lady, all of us parents think all you guys care about is vaccinating."

Ouch, I couldn't believe I'd said that, but I needed to shake her up a bit. And it worked.

"Hey, that's not fair and that's not true."

I said, "Well, then prove it. Get me on the phone with someone who could help get your doctors to sit down with our doctors at this upcoming think tank so we can finally all get on the same page."

She replied, "Okay, I'm going to have someone call you."

I thanked her nicely, hung up the phone, and then dropped to the floor as if someone had just shot me. I was so wickedly exhausted and I realized I might just die an early death from all of this. I looked at Stan and asked him not to leave my room until we got the call. He agreed and I crawled past him on my hands and knees, desperately trying to reach my mattress. I had given that PR woman the last piece of energy I had and needed to lie flat on my bed as soon as possible.

RING RING RING.

WOW! Threatening public humiliation really does make an organization stay on their toes.

The phone continued to ring and I looked at Stan as though all the blood had drained out of my body. I was too physically exhausted to talk to even one more person. I opened Stan's hand and gave him the phone. I put my hand on his shoulder, looked him in the eye, and said, "You can do it."

RING RING RING.

"You really can, Stan. You know more than me. Just speak on my behalf."

Stan nodded his head as if he had been waiting for this moment since his own son's diagnosis. He picked up the phone, lifted it to his ear, and said, "Hello, this is Stan Kurtz. I'm speaking on behalf of Jenny McCarthy."

And the rest is history. I watched Stan on the phone, pacing across the room, for four hours. I was so grateful God sent me a helper, because even though I've got a big mouth and a drive that could move mountains, I am still human. My body can handle only so much.

During the conversation, Stan repeated exactly what we wanted. The man from the AAP began by telling us about his own contributions to the medical establishment since the beginning days of AAP and how far they have come. He was involved in the early research that discovered rubella was associated with certain cases of autism. (Rubella is a live virus, the common European strain of the measles.)

Wait a second. Did this AAP guy just admit that he was involved in early research proving that the rubella virus can cause cases of autism? I couldn't believe it came right out of his mouth that rubella is known to have caused cases of autism. If rubella can cause autism in some children, and moms claim that they lose their children after the MMR vaccine (measles, mumps, and rubella), which has three live viruses including rubella, is it such a huge leap to say that vaccines might trigger autism in some kids?

He also said that in 1999 the AAP put out a public statement that mercury should be removed from vaccines, which is true, but sadly the mercury was not taken out of all the shots. In fact the flu shots still contain traces of mercury, as do all those other shots they claim to have no mercury. And the trace amounts of mercury in them are above the toxic levels for drinking water.

You would think this guy would be totally on our side, right? Not even close.

Stan tried get him back on track and asked him to help organize a group from the AAP to come and sit down with doctors and scientists from Defeat Autism Now! The man on the phone kept diverting the discussion. So Stan kept repeating, "Can you imagine the magnitude of twelve years of information and the help that these kids could get if everyone was just on the same page? Can't we start with common ground? We don't have to talk about metals like mercury or talk about chelation [detox of metals in the body]. Let's just start with diet and vitamins."

The man sighed and said, "Stan, there is no evidence to prove that diet helps autism."

"Yes, there is," Stan said. "There are thousands of parents' testimonies, which are still evidence-based information."

I started silently screaming, IT'S JUST FOOD. IT'S JUST VITAMINS! I personally can't believe the medical community does not support something as simple as diet and vitamins. It just blows my mind. They would be willing to try pharmaceutical mood enhancers on our kids before they would tell them to take dairy out of their diet.

The man then said, "When is this think tank meeting?"

Stan replied, "In about three weeks."

"Oh, no. It's awfully close to a conference we're having on what pediatricians can do to regain the trust of parents, because we are in a crisis of parents not trusting their physicians."

I almost fell off the bed when I heard this and I watched Stan's eyes nearly fall out of his head. Gee, I wonder why there is a crisis between pediatricians and moms. Hmmm...Could it be because they don't listen to us at all and when we have a concern, they make us feel stupid?

The man then went on to say that in their upcoming convention, the AAP will start to encourage pediatricians to talk to parents about their concerns rather than kick them out of their practice for refusing vaccinations for their kids (which has been happening across the country).

I couldn't believe what I was hearing. On the surface it sounded like it could be a positive step, but in reality I knew the goal was simply to find a subtler way to force parents to accept the typical vaccine schedule.

Stan repeated the invitation to the think tank yet AGAIN. "Just please come and listen to what our doctors and scientists have to say. Please. It's helped thousands of kids. Please, sir, please."

The man said, "The doctors you would want to come to this think tank are all working. You're asking me to ask them to take a day off of work. That's a big deal."

A big deal? A day of work? What he said made me so angry that my exhausted body rose from the sheets and I began doing karate around the room, punching and kicking the air. We were asking for someone from the AAP to come and listen to treatments that have been working on thousands of kids for the past twelve years, treatments that could possibly help recover more kids, and his reply was that someone is going to have to miss a day of work? Ugh!

Stan, thank God, kept his peace and said, "Sir, I think it's a small price to pay for something so extraordinary. The information could possibly heal many of these sick kids. I would say that this is worth it."

"I don't know, Stan," the guy said.

Stan and I looked at each other. It was our last resort. We had to use our secret weapon. I waved Stan the go-ahead and Stan said, "Sir, I would much rather come to an agreement tonight before Jenny goes live on *The View* tomorrow morning than to go back and forth like this. We just want one person.... Please.

He replied, "I'll get back to you."

"She goes live at eleven A.M. tomorrow morning. Thank you," Stan said and hung up the phone. We just stood and stared at each other, not knowing whether to rejoice or get mad. The clock was ticking and my mouth was ready to talk on *The View* the next day.

I know that the American Academy of Pediatrics' intentions have been decent through the years. I just believe they are paralyzed by old-school conservative policies and pharmaceutical politics. They are nervous because they really want to see double-blind research before promoting nontraditional treatments like specialized diet and supplements. I can understand their caution, but I would think they would reconsider after years of moms saying, "HEY, IT'S WORKING." The AAP should endorse this group of doctors who are making a difference, or at least sit down for a few days and learn what they're doing. They should support a double-blind placebo study on diet and supplementation, but no one will. WHY? Ugh! It drives me nuts.

6

Nothing Can Stop Me—Not Even Barbara Walters

I WOKE UP the next morning with an upset stomach. I couldn't quite tell if it was from exhaustion, from the phone calls last night, or foreshadowing some trouble in my upcoming press. Today I had to do *The View* and I prayed to God that everything would go smoothly. But judging from my constant running to the bathroom this morning, I had a feeling something was going to go down.

As I was being led to my dressing room at *The View* I glanced back and forth at all the pictures on the walls, of Barbara Walters interviewing some amazing people. I felt so grateful to be interviewing with her today because I grew up watching her. My mom always wanted me to be on her annual year-end show where she interviews famous people. That, or to someday be a Bob Barker beauty on *The Price Is Right*. I had really hoped it wouldn't be the latter, so as a little girl I wished that someday my mom would be able to watch me on *The Barbara Walters Special*.

I entered my dressing room and tried to center myself. I opened my heart and prayed that all my words during the interview would come from love and not ego. I simply wanted to tell my story and represent the voices of thousands of parents who plead for help and change. I noticed a girl who worked at *The View* was walking back and forth past my dressing room, debating whether or not to come in. She looked at me strangely and then came in my room. She had a look of fear all over her face. My stomach dropped because I had a feeling of what she was about to say.

"Jenny, there is some major shit going down. Someone from the network just called Barbara and everyone is going apeshit in the makeup room right now."

"What do you mean?" I replied with a quiver in my voice.

"I guess Barbara is going crazy because you are implying kids are getting cured. Someone from ABC called her just now and said that she has a child with autism and that the treatment you're talking about is bullshit and that kids can't get better on it. That it's not possible."

One thing I have learned in life is to never say anything is impossible. I've lived my life believing that I can make the impossible possible and I wasn't going to let anyone take away that possibility for thousands of mothers.

I felt my heart drop down to my belly button as I continued to listen to this girl talk about how I'm causing a shit storm and might get my ass kicked on TV. I knew it was bound to happen. I knew that such a controversial topic would have to be debated sooner or later. It was hard for me, because even though people might think of me as a ball buster, I'm not really a fighter. I just don't like to fight. So usually when someone tries to argue with me, I say, "Okay, sure, whatever you say." But in this case I knew I couldn't back down. I had to speak up because so many mothers were counting on me. I was really sacred. Really scared. I ran to the bathroom a few more times. I prayed again and just tried to stay centered. I sat back in my dressing room when my segment producer walked in and said to me, "Barbara Walters would like to see you in her dressing room."

WHAT?!

"Okay," I replied confidently. I jumped out of my chair and began walking down the hallway. My heart was beating fast in anticipation of what was about to take place. This is not how I pictured my mother's dream of her daughter being interviewed by Barbara Walters. What do I say to her? What is she gonna say to me? Are we going to wrestle? I didn't know what to expect. I was hoping for a warm, friendly conversation so she could at least get more information about what exactly I'm talking about. That would be wonderful.

I turned the corner and walked into her dressing room. She was getting her makeup done when I said, "Hi, Barbara." She whipped her chair around and sternly stared at me with cold eyes. All I could think was "uh-oh."

"People think you're crazy, you know that?" she said with words made of icicles.

"Um . . . no," I said softly. Then she lowered her chin and managed to lower an octave in her voice and yet raise the volume at the same time.

"MOST doctors do not agree with anything you are saying. Isn't that true?" she said in a wicked, scary tone. I stood there staring at Barbara Walters. I was in shock. Truth be told, I never had anyone yell at me like that—not since Scott Baio heard I called him Chachie in an interview. I took a deep breath and replied, "No, there are plenty of DAN! doctors who have been healing kids through diet and detox that…"

"NO!" she screamed and slowly lifted her pointer finger at me. I watched her face transform into rage. "That's not what I said! I said MOST doctors do NOT agree with anything you're saying! Isn't that true?" I stood frozen with shock and awe yet again. I couldn't believe what was taking place in front of me. I couldn't believe Barbara was so furious about the fact that I had talked about treatments that could heal some kids with autism. Hundreds of doctors have been doing this, but sadly the majority of doctors still didn't know.

I uttered, "Yes, that's true and it's a shame that most doctors don't know about these treatments that are helping these kids. It's also a shame that most doctors don't believe that diet and vitamins can help heal—"

She interrupted me with her yelling voice. "The answer is YES and that is all you're going to say when we get out there and I ask you that question. The answer is YES, most doctors do NOT agree with anything you are saying." I stood there again in shock that someone in journalism I regarded so highly was not only being vicious but also trying to alter what I would say in an interview.

I climbed into my wish bank and quickly erased getting interviewed on the Barbara Walters special for my mom. It was really hard for me to take being yelled at like this when all I was trying to do was offer some hope. I could understand her worry if recovery happened only to one child, but there are more of us. Instead of escalating the situation, I calmly replied, "Yes, ma'am," and walked out of her dressing room. I was scared, hurt, and shocked at this point and wanted to run back home and not do this interview anymore.

When I walked back into my dressing room, everyone in my group was waiting with big eyes and worried faces. The stagehand ran in and said, "We go live in ten minutes. Let's move to the green room." My stomach was in knots. Once we got into the green room, the energy was thick. You had to push the air out of the way because it felt suffocating. Everyone was staring at me with worried eyes. Even the producer put her hand on my shoulder and said, "Oh my God, good luck out there."

Moments later another employee whispered in my ear, "I'm so scared for you."

I knew that whatever happened was meant to happen. I had an overwhelming faith that I couldn't get beaten up because everything I was saying was coming only from love and truth. I wasn't selling a magic potion; I was just offering some hope.

"FIVE, FOUR, THREE, TWO, ONE."

"Our first guest is a *New York Times* bestselling author. Please welcome Jenny McCarthy."

If you happen to see this interview, please look at my terrified eyes at the exact moment Barbara introduces me. Her first question was whether I thought God gives people autism. I had said in my book that I think God chose me to have autism in my life for a reason. That's what I said in my book. But the way she worded it came off completely wrong. In my head I heard, "Oh, shit," but what came out was, "God doesn't give people what they can't handle." Whew. One down. I was still scared out of my mind. I didn't want to fight. I didn't want this to get ugly. Other questions went zooming past me as I numbed my way through the responses. The other women were incredibly sweet and Elizabeth Hasselbeck was really touched. Then finally the moment was here. Barbara asked it. "Jenny, in your book you said that children can get cured."

Everything went into slow motion as I realized something about her question. I realized that Barbara had not yet read the book. That's why she was so upset. If she had read the book, she would have known that not once do I ever say the word "cured." Then I took a deep breath and said, "I agree, there is no cure, but kids can recover." I saw a confused look on her face. I said, "A great example I use [from Stan Kurtz] is that autism is like getting hit by a bus. You cannot become cured from getting hit by a bus, but you can recover!"

Honestly, I can't think of a better scenario than that. After being mowed down by a bus, some people can get up and walk again and others might not be able to. But with the right amount of therapy, some people do recover from such an accident.

Barbara tried her best to ruffle my feathers during the rest of the interview but I stayed focused, stayed within my heart chakra, and just stuck to my story.

The show was over and as I left *The View* that morning all I could think was, "I could really use a big hug from Oprah right now."

7

Home Sweet Home

I WALKED IN THE DOOR, threw my luggage down, and ran to see the little boy who had started all of this in the first place. As I shouted out his name, I got butterflies in my belly. This had been the longest I had ever been away from Evan. Ever! "Evan, Mama's home! Mama's home!" I came around the corner and there he was, staring at me with sad eyes. I said, "Hi, baby! What's wrong?"

He said, "I hate you and I want a new mommy that will stay with me and not go away!" All I could do in that second was think, "What a great sentence!" I got on my knees and told him to come sit on Mama's lap. He slowly walked toward me with his head down and plopped in my lap.

"Evan, I'm so sorry Mommy was gone so long. But someday I'll show you this time in our lives and how it might have helped many kids."

He looked up at me and said, "I'm gonna tell all those kids that it's time to play with Mama now." I laughed and hugged him harder. He's so freaking cute. I can't even stand it sometimes!

People always ask me if Evan understands what happened to him or if he knows what autism is. He doesn't quite get the full concept, but I think most five-year-olds wouldn't. Just a few months ago, though, he did say something extraordinary to me that gave me a glimpse of what Evan remembers from his past.

We were driving home from school and he said, "Mom, I'm not like Dory anymore." (He was referring to Dory the fish in the movie *Finding Nemo*, played by Ellen DeGeneres, who can't remember anything she says.)

I pulled over to the side of the road and said, "What do you mean, Evan?"

As tears welled up in my eyes, he said, "Dory had trouble remembering her words and so did I. Now I don't have trouble with my words anymore. I'm not like Dory!" His smile was so big it almost busted the car windows on both sides.

I cried in awe: All that time my son had been completely aware of his inability to get his words out. It was at that moment I realized that even though our children look completely zoned out, there is actually a spirit inside them that is full of life and love and that needs the same talking to as that of a typical, healthy child. If the child could speak, he or she would say, "Just because I stopped talking, Mom, doesn't mean you should stop. Keep talking to me. I like hearing your voice."

8

The Magnitude of Pain

THAT NEXT WEEK I was scheduled to attend a TACA (Talk About Curing Autism) picnic, which was a gathering of a few thousand families who have children with autism. I asked Evan if he'd like to start coming with me to some of my events. He replied, "You mean...go on an adventure?!" I didn't care if he was going to miss school a few days here and there during this time. I missed out on a lot of bonding time because of autism and now that I got him back I wanted him near me.

When we arrived at the picnic I felt a little nervous in my belly. This would be the first time I would see face-to-face the people I had reached by speaking out. My heart sank as I saw so many families waiting in line, waiting in the hot sun to get an autograph from me. I felt so horrible they had to wait even one second in a line because anyone who has a kid on the autism spectrum knows that our kids DO NOT wait in lines. They go berserk. So I ran to the table, grabbed a pen, and started waving the first family over.

The first mother walked toward me with her child, and my heart completely shattered. She looked into my eyes and locked into my soul. She couldn't speak. Her eyes filled with tears and she told her whole story just by looking at me; her mouth never opened. I nodded to her as if I understood, because I truly did. I lived it. I stood up, put my arms around her, and let her cry. As we stood there hugging I glanced back at the line. They were all looking at me with the same eyes. I knew how important my being there was on this day and I knew these hugs were the best medicine I could give these mommies, but I wasn't sure how much pain I was able to listen to without cracking.

When I got home from this trip, I was greeted with bags of fan mail. My fan mail has ranged from prison inmates to desperate mothers in need. I stared at the bag, not knowing what to do with it. After witnessing the group of mothers at the picnic, I knew these letters were going to bring me to my knees. I knew these women wanted to be heard, so I plopped down on the ground and reached my hand inside the bag of mail. I was just going to read one. Just one. My heart could only handle one this day.

I opened my first letter.

Dear Jenny,

My husband and I watched you on Oprah. We were both watching it feeling so grateful that our son was healthy but our hearts were pouring out to

you and all the other parents that seem to be enduring so much pain. Then you started to speak about
the little things Evan was doing that you didn't
know were signs of autism, like lining up toys, flapping his hands, loss of eye contact. The moment you
started to describe these "characteristics" my husband grabbed my leg and squeezed it. A tear ran
down my cheek because in that moment you had
just diagnosed my son with autism.

Sincerely,
Sarah
Kankakee, IL

I sat there in awe as I held on to this note. I wondered
how many people had learned their child had autism when
they saw me on TV. I wanted to write down the flood of
emotions and thoughts that were racing through my mind
about everything I had gone through and everything that
thousands of parents must be experiencing.

What the HELL happened? How did we all get here?
This is not the image we had with our Cabbage Patch dolls
when we were playing mommy as little girls. This generation of moms are all going through terrible suffering, and
unless you are directly affected by autism, you couldn't
possibly understand the magnitude of pain these moms are
enduring.

People need to realize it's not *just* genetics. Genetics go
from one generation to the next. This is an epidemic that has
taken over on such a massive scale that it pains me to no end

that they think it's one gene that's causing this. I believe there are genetic vulnerabilities that affect how we are able to process environmental toxins, just like there might be genetic vulnerabilities to skin cancer from sun exposure or lung cancer from smoking. Not everyone will get lung cancer from smoking, but some are certainly more predisposed than others. I believe there are genetic vulnerabilities for one out of ninety-four boys right now who can't handle the toxins in vaccines and the environment, so it's triggering autism.

If a child is born with an infection that no one can see and we vaccinate them while their immune system cannot sufficiently fight the toxins or viruses being injected, that child is going to get into trouble. The same holds true when you take your kid to get their shots and the doctor says he can't immunize because the child is sick. The child needs to get well and then get the shots. And why is that, Doc?

He or she would say because the immune system is under attack or fighting something else and can't handle the shot. So can we please assume that some children are born with an infection or yeast overload or maybe a mitochondrial issue and can't handle the first shot they are given in the hospital? Can we assume that some kids could be born perfectly healthy but vaccines then damage the mitochondria, which then could trigger autism? Can we assume that some kids are more vulnerable to toxic overloads than are others? Can we assume that some children can't handle ALL thirty-six shots?

You're damn right we should assume this. It's INSANE that hospitals think that EVERY child is born perfect, that

EVERY child has a perfect immune system, and that a history of autoimmune problems in families doesn't mean anything.

There needs to be a test for newborns to see if they are free from infection and fungus. We also need to make sure the child's glutathione levels are high. (Glutathione is a natural antioxidant in the body.) If a child has low glutathione, which most kids with autism have, we should have the brains not to vaccinate.

We need the American Academy of Pediatrics to get off its butt and focus on alleviating the fears and concerns we the parents in this country have. Stop trying to prove us wrong and just listen to us!

9

Speaking of the Devil

THE AAP AGREED to come to the DAN! conference! Hooray! Then again maybe not.

DAN! (Defeat Autism Now!) is an organization of doctors and scientists who are the medical leaders in healing children with autism. I know it has a weird name and acronym, but don't let that keep you from coming. I remember the first time I heard someone say, "Get a DAN! doctor." All I could think was, "How do I find this guy Dan?"

DAN! holds many conferences a year. There's at least one on the East Coast and one on the West Coast. EVERY parent who has a child with autism MUST get there. Get there this year. Don't wait any longer!

This is the conference I invited the American Academy of Pediatrics to, and guess what? They sent someone. They really sent someone! I was nervous and hoped to God that whoever came would have an open mind and heart. A female doctor came into the room with a big smile and sweet eyes. We sat down with the senior doctors from DAN!, who pleaded with this AAP doctor to begin taking a look at all the research they have and to recognize common health ailments in kids with autism. They explained to the AAP doctor that kids can get better and that they *are* getting better and if they teach this to pediatricians across the country, they could save many lives.

I watched the female doctor from the AAP talk and tried to read her mind. I could tell she had compassion for us, but her beating around the bush was starting to annoy me. In a nutshell she was telling us that if it's not in their medical journal or their new tool kit they give to pediatricians, then nothing can be done. She told us to write a note to the AAP explaining our findings and she apologized that she couldn't stay for the rest of the conference.

I couldn't believe she was telling us to write a letter. As I sat there with my mouth hanging open, I was in complete awe that a medical organization would not sit down and talk to doctors who are healing an epidemic. What the hell kind of country is this? These kids are so sick and the American Academy of Pediatrics wants us to write them a letter? Shame on them. Shame…on…them.

She went on to tell us to say in the letter that these conditions are comorbid with autism, not that these conditions cause autism. I sat there dumbfounded and leaned over to ask Stan, "What the hell are comorbid conditions?" It turns out "comorbid" means that the conditions exist simultaneously with autism, but are not causal. Stan scribbled down on a piece of paper, "Stuff like leaky gut, infections, and toxins." I sat there puzzled, because once I had fixed Evan's comorbid conditions, the autism healed. So she was asking us to cleverly disguise what we believe by saying that these conditions have nothing to do with the cause of autism. Essentially she asked us to lie. These comorbid conditions clearly stem from vaccines, and God forbid we say comorbid conditions cause autism, because that would be a direct link to vaccines.

She then told us that a new "autism tool kit" (which is a bunch of pieces of paper that tell pediatricians how to diagnose and treat kids with autism and how to find earlier warning signs) was coming out and that we would be happy with the updates they put in it. The DAN! doctors all looked at each other, fearing that this tool kit would offer nothing on how to treat these "comorbid conditions" in children with autism. We shook her hand and she left to board a plane. I prayed to God that all this work to get them to this conference would at least make something happen on their side.

10

At This Moment in Time, the American Academy of Pediatrics Sucks

I REALIZED HOW FAR AWAY we were from getting the AAP to recognize and treat ailments associated with autism. My realization came months after the conference, when I learned that nothing had been implemented from our meeting. No progress whatsoever. I realized that my work was far from over and knew that the only way to change anything is to change the community itself. I needed to get out and keep talking about it in the hopes that people would listen and start demanding help with me. I couldn't do this by myself anymore.

I continued on the road, hitting city after city, and was greeted by the same faces: faces of heartache, fear, debt, feeling alone, and anger. I wish to God I could have brought a member of the CDC and the AAP with me on this tour because being on the front line is really the only way to truly feel the magnitude of the suffering going on across the country. I listened to story after story, and every story was the same: "I vaccinated my kid and something happened to him because then he stopped speaking." I stood on stages and looked out into the crowds of moms who were all screaming the same thing, "Someone listen to us!"

It was during this time on tour I started to crack. I was becoming so overwhelmed with everyone's stories. I felt obligated to listen to all of them because they needed to be heard, too. They needed an outlet and I was the one they wanted to tell their stories to. Listening to their stories, I began to realize how strong these women are. Some of them had four children with autism, some of them with fifteen-year-olds still in diapers. But what was so amazing about them all was their strength and determination to never give up.

I realized that people needed to hear these stories of healing. Since the AAP is years away from recognizing how we are making our kids feel better, it is up to the mothers of this generation to teach other mothers. These mothers have stories that offer hope, faith, and lessons in love. After meeting and hearing thousands of them, here are the mother warriors I need you to hear.

PART TWO

Strength in Numbers

11

Michelle Woods: Mother Warrior to Kevin

I MET MICHELLE at an autism conference in Atlanta. She came charging toward me with a look of determination on her face. She was the kind of girl you wouldn't think would have the strongest armor, but I took one look into those eyes of hers and I knew I was in the presence of a warrior. She moved through the crowd and held a DVD up to me. "I recovered my kid and I have a story to tell," she yelled.

I went back to my hotel room and watched her DVD. It was a video chronicle of her and her son through the years. I heard the determination in her voice as she talked to her son while he obviously didn't even know she was there. I watched her go through this time alone, with no husband to support her, which is sadly too common. I watched as her son progressed from nonresponsiveness to saying a few words and then to talking conversations. Her son had so many health issues that it was a miracle he had any improvement at all. The fact that he recovered was amazing even to me. After watching the DVD she had so proudly shared with me, and after listening to her story, I knew she had all the qualifications of a Mother Warrior. So I give you her story.

ON THE DAY OF DIAGNOSIS, I took Kevin in to the TEACCH Center, which is based at the University of North Carolina at Chapel Hill. He was nineteen months old. The evaluation was very hard for me because Kevin, up to that point, had never really been separated from me. They took him and put him in a room by himself with the evaluators and they put my ex-husband and me in another room. While they were interviewing us to find out about what Kevin was doing at home, we could hear him screaming in the next room. It sounded as if he was being tortured. It was so traumatic for me because here's a kid who is sick and miserable anyway and then you put him in a room with strangers. It was torture.

HEARING MICHELLE TALK about Kevin's first evaluation reminded me of the sadness I felt during Evan's initial evaluation. I remembered how my heart felt like it was being ripped out, not only from hearing Evan scream in the other room but from the hell of watching him fail test after test behind a two-way mirror. I then asked Michelle if she suspected it was autism at this first evaluation.

I HAD SUSPECTED IT just based on talking with my pediatrician. Kevin had so much good development in the
beginning and then he lost so much of it. He got really sick
really fast, and as soon as he started getting sick with all of
his autoimmune stuff, that's when he lost his developmental
milestones. And so it looked to me like autism, but at that
point I didn't know anything about the neuroimmune connection. So I went in expecting to get a diagnosis but not expecting it to be that bad.

They tested his IQ and it was something like 60 or 70.
Here's a kid who was talking when he was just a few months
old, here's a kid who had his developmental milestones way
ahead of the norm and then...just lost everything.

I started to notice the changes when Kevin was about six
months old and it was near Christmas 2002. That's when he
got his DTaP vaccine (diphtheria, tetanus, pertussis) with
the Hib vaccine (Hib disease), and right after that he started
losing everything. He began getting really sick and lost all of
his milestones. He had eczema all over his body, he started
to bleed internally. He was anemic and the pediatrician said
maybe it's too much milk. And I said, "Well, I don't really
think I give him that much milk, but I'll take your word for
it and give him some iron supplements and cut down on the
milk." As it turns out, it didn't have anything to do with the
milk. He was bleeding so much. He was losing iron.

He was bleeding in his colon and his small intestine and
it was getting worse and worse. So they did a colonoscopy

and endoscopy with biopsies and they found that he had lymphoid nodular hyperplasia in his colon. Our lymph system is related to our immune system, and lymph nodules in the colon get inflamed. Hyperplasia means the nodules are bigger than they are supposed to be and they become inflamed when there is an immune reaction. Kevin's were inflamed to the point that every time he was eating they were bleeding. So everything he ate hurt him. He also had gastritis, inflammation in the stomach. With all that inflammation, you are going to bleed profusely, and he did. I had to watch my son in chronic gastrointestinal pain. It was killing me, and their solution was to do nothing. It was so frustrating.

You know, you have all of these hopes and dreams for your child. Everybody does. Even if we don't admit it, we all have expectations that our children will be healthy and happy, at the very least. And when you have a child who is sick and who is then diagnosed with autism, it's devastating. You feel absolutely helpless. It's like opening a whole new world of unknowns: I don't know how to fix this, I don't know how to help him, and I don't know how to make him feel better. I don't know how to get him back on track so that he can be a happy, healthy, normal kid. And, as somebody who is accustomed to taking problems and tackling them, it's very difficult as a mother to know there's nothing you can do or to be told there's nothing you can do.

At the evaluation, they told me that there was not much I could do other than behavioral interventions, occupational therapy, speech therapy, things like that. The day we got the diagnosis, I had no idea that Kevin's autism was medically based. Nobody mentioned anything to me about immune deficiency or immune reactions or environmental toxins or anything like that. That was a world opened up to me later. But when he got his diagnosis, the only thing they were telling us we could do was start teaching him how to behave, essentially rewiring his behavioral networks so that he understands how to cope with stressful or anxiety-provoking situations. Kevin was so physically ill at this exact same time, I wish someone had told me that it was related!

I talked to my local gastroenterologist about Kevin's lymphoid nodular hyperplasia and he said I could go the route of steroids, but in a child this young it's really not typical. I left there looking at my boy and knowing it was up to me to help him. I had to figure it out on my own. So I went home, got on the Internet, and Googled "lymphoid nodular hyperplasia and autism."

My life would have been totally different if I had typed it in a different way. But something inside me, my instinct, made me type in "lymphoid nodular hyperplasia AND autism." I had no idea there was a connection. Then up came Dr. Arthur Krigsman on my Google search. And there in front of me was the connection I had no idea existed and was about to save Kevin's life. After I found Dr. Krigsman, everything started to get better.

THE CONFIDENCE in Michelle's voice took my breath away. There was nothing in her tone that suggested she was a victim. With every word she spoke, I was inspired and wanted to know even more about her. I noticed that she hadn't mentioned much about her husband and I wondered what was going on in her marriage at this point.

My husband's interpretation of this was "you go and do what you want to do. I'll be at work, working on my career." The thing that frustrated me and hurt me so much about his attitude was that I had a career, too. Our child got sick and things needed to be adjusted.

Prior to the diagnosis I was a tenure-track professor. I had my first professorship when I was twenty-four years old. I was one of the youngest professors ever at the university where I worked and maybe one of the youngest professors ever in the field of anthropology. That's my specialty, life histories and cultural anthropology. My dissertation won awards and I published articles. I even wrote a book and submitted it for review. When Kevin got sick, that was it. That was the end of that track. When you have a sick child, everything else becomes moot.

My son needed help and I felt that if I had the ability to make this better, then it was my responsibility to do so. So I rearranged my burgeoning career so I could teach all online classes, which would allow me to be at home healing Kevin.

I knew I had to keep some aspect of my identity intact, and continuing to work during this time did just that. I didn't want to lose myself completely, which is so easy to do when you have a child on the autism spectrum. I never wanted to have a reason to be resentful or bitter later in life.

And then I found Dr. Krigsman, and he started Kevin on a gluten-free and casein-free diet. But that didn't work for Kevin. There wasn't anything left for the kid to eat because he was allergic to everything—and I'm not exaggerating. The only thing he wasn't allergic to was wheat. We were up a creek because the kid's got to have some kind of nourishment. We didn't want to put him on a G-tube. I absolutely refused to do that because I said I would teach my child how to eat. He didn't want to eat anything at all. He didn't want to chew. He didn't want to swallow. So then we started occupational therapy to help him learn how to eat. And we started him on sulfasalazine to try to calm all the inflammation in his gut.

After I talked to Dr. Krigsman, he said go to a DAN! conference and get involved there. And I guess Dr. Krigsman must've known from talking to me that I'm the kind of person who is going to fight to the very end to get my kid back on track.

So I went to the DAN! conference and that was it. Everything was different from then on. All of these parents were saying the same thing there. They had the exact same experience that I had with Kevin, and their kids were getting better. And the doctors there were not witch doctors. These were not people who were trying to take advantage of parents. These were not people who were trying to make a buck. These were people who were doing real research at real universities. And I, coming from a university, had a particular perspective on that. I know how hard it is to get papers published by peer-reviewed journals, and if their research was good enough to get reviewed by their peers and published in respectable journals, then it was real research. You can't debate the fact that the real research they were doing was pointing to a connection between the immune system and autism. Once I saw that and once I realized that they aren't out to take advantage of parents, they aren't out to sell snake oil, they're out to help kids, it was a huge turning point for me.

I knew I needed to learn everything I could about this to try to put the pieces together and figure out what was wrong with Kevin because he was already starting to get better with the sulfasalazine. It was baby steps. Every now and then he would improve and get something at a faster rate than he was with the behavioral interventions alone. I think biomedical therapies not only helped him to feel better but really helped him to make those neurological connections. When I saw Dr. James Neubrander speak at the DAN! conference, I ran home and called him. The man wasn't even back from the conference yet and I called his office and said, "I need an appointment with Dr. Neubrander because I want methyl B12 for my son."

At that point I didn't know. It was more an intuition because in my family, there is a history of pernicious anemia, which is an inability to process B12 from food. I have first cousins who get injections of B12 regularly. And that's why, when I went to the conference about methyl B12, I said, "Aha, maybe there's a connection."

I called the office and I got the methyl B12 shots. I gave Kevin the first methyl B12 shot and, I kid you not, he was like a totally different boy the day after he had his shot. The teacher came up to me and said, "What did you do with this kid? Because this is not the kid we had in here yesterday."

I said, "Tell me what you see. Tell me what you're seeing in class."

She said, "He's not pushing anybody, he's not screaming, he's sitting down, he's doing his work, he's happy, he's laughing, he's making jokes. What did you do to this kid?"

And that's when I knew that he had a methyl B12 deficiency...because I had never supplemented him with B12 before then.

At that point, I was giving it to him once every three days. And the teachers could tell the day after he had his shot because it would wear off gradually. By the second or third day, he was back to his old self, back to his sick, bad-behavior self. And so I called Dr. Neubrander and said, "Look, you've got to do something for me here because this boy is responding to the methyl B12, but only after the first day. It wears off too fast." That's when Dr. Neubrander put him on the shots every day and that's when Kevin started to get better.

With the methyl B12 shots, we saw tremendous social improvement. Not necessarily cognitive improvements (those didn't come until the hyperbaric oxygen) but tremendous social ability. He was such a fun-loving kid when he started on the shots. He loved life and he would laugh and play with other kids. He would extend himself to other kids to make friends.

Then Dr. Neubrander moved me to hyperbaric oxygen (therapy that uses high-pressured oxygen, usually in a chamber). I didn't start it right away. Part of the reason it took me a little while to get into hyperbaric is because I wanted to see physically, medically, why it worked. There is a stigma of autism moms being willing to try anything and I will try something as long as there is a real basis to it. So I researched it and found that hyperbaric oxygen has been used for years, for wound healing, to suppress inflammation, and to help with autoimmune diseases like rheumatoid arthritis and lupus. I have lupus, so I thought this is a connection, this is yet another piece of the puzzle.

We did a total of fifteen hours in the tank, and within forty-eight hours, Kevin was a different child. That's when he hit the ground running. His teachers said that all of a sudden he was doing math work and was talking more. He was engaging more. He was using more eye contact. He was actually taking initiative. He was telling the teachers what he wanted, and his thinking process was just faster. The connections they hadn't seen before were there now.

There's a tremendous amount of guilt and responsibility that goes with being an autism mom because you're the one making all the decisions. My ex-husband didn't want to have anything to do with it. He basically said, "Whatever you think, go ahead." So it's all on us moms to heal our children from this "incurable disease." Nothing like a little bit of pressure to start your day. So basically, I would wake up in the morning and check in with Kevin and make sure he hadn't regressed from the day before. If he was doing okay, then I could get through my day. But the worst days were when he would get sick with a cold or something, because every time he got sick he would regress.

I TOLD MICHELLE how I could relate to her experience. Every time Evan gets sick, even to this day, it's as if the autism returns. Regression is one of the most common fears, if not the single most fear that parents of children with autism face. We never want to see them go backward. We wake up every day and go through our morning checklist to make sure nothing was lost. When they get sick, they usually do regress.

FOR SOME REASON, moms take it personally when their children regress. At least I did. I got pissed because I had gone through all this freaking work and now my kid is regressing? No! I'm not going to let this happen. And I'd get really angry and really nervous because what if it's permanent? But thankfully, he came back every time and continued to move forward.

We also started him on 6-MP, which is mercaptopurine; it helps with inflammation in the gut. It really helped to get his blood levels under control because his white blood cell count was so high. His ear doctor did tests for eosinophils (white blood cells) and said it was the highest level of eosinophils she had ever seen in all her years of practicing medicine. His immune response was off the charts.

Kevin is five now and he goes to public school kindergarten, with no services and no shadow. So here's a kid who had no words, had an IQ of 70, and was clearly autistic.

Today you would never know that autism was in his history. His kindergarten teacher says he's at or above grade level in all of his academics. She said, "You know he has some problems with his speech."

I responded, "Okay, yeah, we're working on that." I laughed because we entered Kevin in school with no diagnosis and no one knew. My ex-husband didn't want me to tell anybody that he was autistic because, sadly, my ex-husband was embarrassed about Kevin's autism. Once I fixed the autism, it was easy for him to pass Kevin off as normal. Just a little speech problem was all they saw at school. I've never been embarrassed about Kevin's autism. I've always been just the opposite. Here is something you can do to help your kid, but because my ex-husband shares legal custody, I couldn't show his face. It was a good Christmas, though. My divorce became final and my boy is all better. Two things to be incredibly grateful for.

Now that he's doing better, it feels like I've been introducing myself to him all over again. He was so sick his whole life. I didn't have time to get to know him when he was little because after he got that six-month vaccination, he was gone. And so I only had six months to get to know him. Here I am, reintroducing myself to this child who's been there all this time but has been masked by all the immune system stuff, and by the autism.

It's very difficult to explain to somebody who does not have a special needs child how much hope we really have. We have enough hope for everyone around us, and you have to believe in yourself enough to be able to do it, to get it done.

You have to be able to face doctors who will tell you you're crazy because you don't believe in the vaccine program and that you think everything they are saying is bunk. You have to be strong enough not to believe them when they're telling you there's nothing you can do for your kid. You have to be able to have enough hope and to believe in yourself enough to combat that and to go home at the end of the day and say, "I know I'm right." You have to be strong enough to look at them and say, "I know my child better than anybody else and I know that I will be able to heal this child." You have to be willing to stand up to the criticism. Anybody who's ever done anything great has had to do that. I think all of us who have healed our kids know that you have to put up with a lot of crap to be able to do it.

There's nothing more hopeless than when doctors tell you they can't fix the brain because they can't get to it. It's like hearing, "Sorry, something's screwed up in their brain. Have a nice day." But if it's something in their gut or their immune system or their blood, you can fix that. As a mom it gives you hope to know that it's not just something inherently wrong with your kid, which is how they portrayed it for so long. First it was refrigerator moms and then it was, "Well, you know, he must have bumped his head on the way out." No, it's not that. It's something totally different and it's something totally fixable. It gave me tremendous hope to learn that if I fix his gut and fix his immune system, maybe he'll get better. And he did. He just happened to be a child who did get better.

A diagnosis of autism is no longer the death sentence it

used to be. It's like any other disease; it takes a while for medicine to catch up. It takes a while for the community to catch up to the science. And the science says this is an autoimmune disease and manifests behaviorally as autism. If you treat it as an autoimmune disease or as a neuroimmune disease, then kids will get better. They may not be completely healed, but they will get better, and that's better than doing nothing, for God's sake. You've got to get out and try.

12

Canaries in the Coal Mine

"CANARIES IN THE COAL MINE" is a saying often used in the autism community and I can't think of a better analogy than this.

The saying comes from a longtime practice of coal miners in England and the United States. The miners would go down into the mines with a caged canary to serve as an early warning of the presence of methane and carbon monoxide gas. Canaries are especially sensitive to the gases; if the canary weakened or died, the miners fled the mine.

There is such a similarity with autistic kids. Children with autism are our little canaries. Their sensitivity is much more acute than ours. Just like the canaries, you know these kids are going to get sick first. They're the ones who are the most susceptible to toxins and they have been increasing in greater numbers every year. Their warnings are showing us what we don't see in ourselves yet.

I look at the older generation right now and the rise of

Alzheimer's, Parkinson's, MS. Then I look at this young generation and see autism, ADD, ADHD, allergies, childhood diabetes, and Tourette's and wonder what our future will look like when my generation grows old. If before us is Alzheimer's and Parkinson's and behind us are all of these other diseases and disabilities, shouldn't we be a little worried about what the hell we're gonna get?

These children are trying so hard to show us how to live in a cleaner world. I believe these kids are here for a reason: to teach us to eat better, clean up the air, and get rid of toxins because they can't survive. Everyone, not just mothers who have kids with autism, needs to pay serious attention to their warning. I know this is their main purpose and pray that we all start to wake up and collectively change this world into the new world our kids are working so hard to create. Listen for their "tweet, tweet" because these canaries will save the world.

13

Amazing Maisie

Dear Jenny,

Before my daughter had autism, I thought people were generally good. I thought doctors were experts whose advice should be followed. I thought the government, while obviously a little screwed up, was really looking out for the interests and welfare of the people. I believed that vaccines were safe and that kids were lucky to be born in a time when there were so many diseases that could be prevented with a little shot in the arm. Jenny, I was wrong.

My daughter Maisie was born in 2001. This same year the Institute of Medicine, a component of the National Academy of Sciences, met to discuss vaccine safety and the mercury-based preservative thimerosal. At this meeting, doctors and researchers discussed how much mercury was contained in the shots that American children were getting. They talked about the relationship between mercury and autism, ADHD, and language delays. Then they decided that "full consideration be given to removing thimerosal from any biological product to which infants, children, and pregnant women are exposed." However, they decided not to recall any mercury-containing vaccines, require doctors to disclose that they were giving shots with mercury, or require drug companies to make safer vaccines. Maisie received fifteen vaccines in her first nine months of life. All of them were made in 1998 or 1999. All of them contained mercury.

On Maisie's first birthday, I pulled out her baby book and wrote. I wrote about the words Maisie had learned, "Mama," "Dada," "ball," "more." Maisie had thirteen words that she was saying often and appropriately. I wrote that she had learned six baby signs, too. She could competently sign "all done," "Where?," "mine," and others. I wrote that Maisie had started walking the month before and enjoyed toddling after her sister, chasing our tolerant cat, and racing to the door when her dad came home. I wrote about playing peek-a-boo and reading with her and how much she enjoyed that hour before bedtime when her older sister would get silly with her and they'd run laps around the house, giggling and chasing until I captured them for a story and a cuddle. I'm so glad I took the time to write it all. Maisie's life was about to become very different.

Two days after Maisie's birthday, we went to the doctor for a "well child" checkup. Maisie was growing and developing exactly on schedule and was happy and charming during the visit. Until it was time for her shots. At this checkup Maisie was to get just two shots. These two shots contained four live viruses: measles, mumps, rubella, and chicken pox. I laid Maisie down on the exam table with one arm across her chest and my other hand pinning her legs down and still. I tried to speak reassuringly to my child as the nurse swabbed her thighs with alcohol and jabbed the needles in. Our children trust us to keep them safe. I thought that the shots and the pain and treachery of holding Maisie down for them were necessary evils to prevent her from further harm. I thought I was doing the right thing.

Within a week, Maisie developed a fever. I blew it off as one of those "mild vaccines reactions" and didn't worry about it. By the next week the fever had broken, but I noticed Maisie wasn't saying much anymore. I waited another couple of weeks before taking her to the doctor. She was saying only about three words, and randomly, not appropriately. The doctor blew me off: "She's just working on other skills; don't worry about it." We went back a couple months later for another "well baby" checkup. Maisie still wasn't talking. I asked about the vaccine-autism connection and told the doctor I was worried about giving more shots. The doctor looked at me like I was crazy and strongly denied the idea that vaccines could cause autism. Against my better judgment and every mothering instinct I had, I backed down. The nurse brought in the needles and once again, I held my baby down to receive them. Three shots, all containing mercury.

Now the spiral started. Maisie stopped playing, she stopped looking at us, the few words she had left disappeared. The odd behavior began: spinning, flapping, opening and closing cupboard doors with a frantic bangity-bangity-bang rhythm, wedging herself into tight spaces under furniture, between the bed and the wall, inside a cabinet. Worst of all, the Maisie from her baby book vanished. There was still a child who required feeding, washing, and minding, but there was no soul in that child. She was invisible. I didn't know what she liked, what she wanted, what she thought. She didn't laugh or play games. Maisie was gone. I didn't know what happened or what to do.

One day while waiting in the lobby of my older daughter's preschool, I noticed the school director watching Maisie as she flapped her hands and chanted a low rhythm of "ya ya ya ya" to herself. Catching my eye, she bravely spoke: "Those often are autistic behaviors. Have you had her evaluated?" I still hadn't been able to get the pediatrician to say anything was wrong, but this confirmed my nagging suspicions. The school director gave me the number of another mother at the school who had a child with autism and encouraged me to call her.

I tried to think of reasons not to call. I feel so awkward calling people up randomly, and what was this person going to say anyway? For some reason, though, I found myself dialing the phone one day. The woman I talked to was amazing! She gave me the Web sites for the Autism Research Institute, a Listserv called autism-mercury, and books to read, and she filled my head over the next hour with information about vaccines, autism, mercury, treatments, and research.

When I got off the phone I was unstoppable. I was going to fix this. I was going to shove my way into the Land of Autism and yank my daughter back out. I was mad and I channeled all that angry Mom energy into fighting for my kiddo. I showed up at the doctor's office and demanded a copy of Maisie's vaccine records. I spent hours online reading, researching, and e-mailing other parents I found, asking for help and to share what they were doing for their kids. I went to the library and calculated how much mercury Maisie got in her shots, using the vaccine info from the doctor and the *Physician's Desk Reference* from the years the shots were made. I found a list on the Autism Research Institute Web site of DAN! practitioners, doctors who were treating autism, and called everyone in my area. I wanted to know if they treated mercury poisoning and if they had ever treated a child as young as mine. Maisie was eighteen months old. I hoped that if I could get the mercury out soon, while she was still so young, maybe just maybe she'd come back to us. I found a doctor who sounded promising, and off we went to our first appointment.

And so it began. Gluten-free, casein-free (GFCF) diet, vitamin supplements, blood draws, urine collections, stinky medicine ground up and hidden in rice-milk ice cream. Every treatment saw results. Some were amazingly good! The first week on the GFCF diet, Maisie started talking. Some treatments were not as nice. TMG (tri-methyl-glycine), which works great for some kids, made Maisie crazy and she went on a light-switch-flipping, cupboard-door-banging freak-out for three days. I ignored how much money treatments, therapy, and lab tests cost. I decided I would gladly give up our house before I'd give up on my little girl.

Maisie was diagnosed with Autism Spectrum Disorder (ASD) at age two. Five months later we had started her on the GFCF diet. She had learned more than fifty words by then, but her use of language and her social delays were unquestionable. One year later and eighteen months after starting biomedical interventions and supplementing with many, many hours of behavior therapy, Maisie was "undiagnosed" by the developmental pediatrician, speech language pathologist, and psychologist who had originally evaluated her. These professionals were quite skeptical that Maisie could have recovered from an "untreatable disorder," but after reviewing the tape they'd made of her the year before, they concluded that she was not simply "misdiagnosed." They were completely astounded. Maisie's only remaining issue at that time was her speech, which could be difficult to understand. One more year of speech therapy fixed that, and Maisie graduated from all special service and support.

Today, Maisie is indistinguishable from her peers. She has a best friend. She plays softball. She lost her first tooth and rejoiced in finding the dollar bill left by the tooth fairy. She's almost mastered riding her bike without training wheels. She wants to go to Hawaii and see Jimmy Buffett in concert some day. She talks about her day at school, what she likes, who she played with, why she got mad and hit the little girl who was teasing her at recess. She is a charming, stubborn, silly, sweet, typical kid. I wonder sometimes what she would have been like had she not been captured by autism. I wonder what she remembers about those years. I asked her once if she remembered what it was like when she didn't talk. Maisie thought for a minute and then said loudly and clearly, "I remember. But I'm glad I can talk now!"

I'm grateful to all the mothers who paved the way, answered my e-mails, and fought for their children before me. They got me going. I'm grateful to the mothers who fought alongside me and kept me company in line at the health food stores and in the lobby of the therapy clinics. They held me up. And I'm grateful to you, Jenny, for keeping the fight going, for moving it into the studios of Oprah and Larry King, for being loud and spreading the word. Autistic kids can get better. We will continue to fight for them.

With much love,
Melanie Glock

14

Lisa Ackerman: Mother Warrior to Jeff

WITHIN A FEW MONTHS of Evan getting diagnosed, an autism mom came up to me and said, "You need to talk to Lisa Ackerman."

"Who the hell is Lisa Ackerman?"

The mom smiled coyly at me and said, "She is the Yoda of autism moms. She knows everything about autism. She knows every doctor and every treatment available and knocks down any door to get what she wants. She's the one that can show you the way."

Within minutes I was on the phone with Lisa. She told me her story and how she had not yet recovered her son but that he had made incredible strides and she would never give up trying. She created a support group called TACA (Talk About Curing Autism) for families who have children with autism, and I bow my head to her for guiding thousands of families through some pretty rough roads. Here is her story.

I MET MY SECOND HUSBAND, Glen, by almost hitting him with my car. He was a pedestrian. I wasn't. I yelled "sorry about that" and we started seeing each other.

Eventually we got married and started a business together. After nine years of hard work, I walked down the stairs one day and said, "What happened? We were supposed to have two kids." Nine months later, Jeff was born, weighing in at a perfect seven pounds one ounce. I knew it was going to be a boy because I had told Glen, "You need a little mini me." And Jeff turned out to be exactly like that. Both of their baby pictures look identical.

Jeff's first word was of course "dada" because the connection that Jeff and Glen had was unbelievably beautiful. The only thing separating these two was a little bit of air; other than that, they were one person. He sat up on time, crawled, did everything the baby books said he would.

The setback and changes began on June 1, 1999. That's the day Jeff received the varicella (chicken pox) and MMR (measles, mumps, rubella) vaccines in the same day. It was as if someone had wiped out his brain. We went in that day for his well-baby checkup and to get his shots. Jeff had been on antibiotics at the time, fighting his sixth ear infection. I had no idea that you are not supposed to give children vaccines when they are sick or have a cold or are on antibiotics because the body cannot handle another type of assault.

Not knowing that Tylenol lowers glutathione (the body's natural antioxidant), I also gave him Tylenol before we went in so the shot wouldn't hurt as much. So let's just review what was going on in Jeff's body at this point. He was fighting a cold that was all bacterial and on antibiotics, so his immune system was weakened; then we gave him Tylenol and then added a quadruple live virus to him. The chances of getting through that are probably not so good. There's not a good chance that a person will come out the other side without an effect on the gut or immune system.

When we went home from the doctor's that same day, Glen came up to me and said, "That's strange. Usually, Jeff throws a fit when we give him the antibiotics and kicks and screams and spits it out." Giving him antibiotics was always a major ordeal. On that day, he didn't even respond. I put it in his mouth and...nothing.

Around this time Jeff had twelve to twenty words and approximations. As the weeks went on, these words slowly disappeared and so did other achieved milestones. He also started to become really cranky all the time. Something was bothering him. This was followed by his no longer sleeping through the night, along with frequent nighttime vomiting. He started staring like a zombie at the television, toe walking, becoming fascinated with spinning objects, and eating sand at the park. He was insensitive to heat, cold, or things that should cause pain, yet he couldn't tolerate a tag in his clothes or a small thread out of place. And then the full-body rashes began. The rashes appeared to be "mobile" on his body. When I inquired about the rashes at his summer well-baby checkup, the doctor said it was a heat rash.

Jeff then went from eating everything to eating only five

items. When we went to see our pediatrician, his associate was filling in that day. We told her about all these things (the disappearance of skills and words, loss of sleep, rashes), and she looked over at Jeff and started calling his name. "Jeff. Jeff!" she said. Nothing. Jeff didn't respond at all. She looked back at me and said, "Can you get Jeff's attention right now?"

Then I tried, "Jeff. Jeff. Jeff!" Nothing. A response that was becoming usual. I needed to physically move him to get his attention. She recommended that we get his hearing and speech checked.

His hearing came back fine, but his speech evaluation came back as that of a zero to three-month-old. He was two and a half! It was like someone had thrown a bucket of water on me. I couldn't believe it. The speech pathologist then sent us to a neurologist. Before the appointment, I went online and researched symptomology, sounding or acting deaf, loss of language, and up came the National Institute of Mental Health: Autism. It said the symptoms for autism are self-injurious behavior, rocking in a corner, and flapping in front of the eyes. It didn't seem like a connection to me, because Jeff had no self-injury, he didn't rock, and he flapped only when he got excited but not in front of his eyes. I thought to myself that he doesn't match this, but he did match the loss of speech and acting deaf.

Finally we were getting our neurological assessment done and Jeff was freaking out! He was crying and wouldn't pay attention. And all we kept thinking was, "You're torturing him!"

When the evaluation ended, the man said, "I'm pretty sure it's autism. There really isn't a cure. There is nothing you can do except maybe get Jeff some behavioral support so you and your husband can get on with your lives."

The sound in the room had stopped. Everything around me went into slow motion and I went into shock. But not like a bad-car-accident shock. It was different. It was a numbing, a shutdown of any emotions I once had. It took two days for me to look at my husband or even say a word to him. We were zombies walking through the house. My daughter, Lauren, was the first person who got me to cry. I explained to her that there was no treatment and she replied, "Bullshit." That made me cry. She pressed the button.

But I still couldn't talk to Glen. There was a wall and it was named avoidance. When we did speak to each other it was "just the facts, please." We worked together and everything was business only and whenever we did talk, all I said was "We need this done. We need that done." That was it. I felt like I was on an island by myself dealing with the worst thing in the whole world. And being raised Irish Catholic, I thought that if you don't look at it, it doesn't exist. So I would constantly tell myself, "Don't look at it, don't look at it, don't look at it!"

My friends at the time didn't want to hang around because Jeff was such an animal. He would destroy their houses. He was like the Tasmanian devil. He was unpredictable and no one could interact with him—except his dad. I didn't really call my brothers and sisters, because they had perfect children. The last thing I wanted to do was talk to someone who had perfect kids and didn't understand what I was going through. So I continued to avoid the hurt, telling myself, "Don't go there. Don't go there."

After four months of stalling and delaying by the regional autism center, we finally got services. Jeff was three now and we started him on twenty-five hours of services a week. At this time, Jeff was receiving ABA (applied behavior analysis), speech, and OT (occupational therapy) services—no biomedical intervention.

My husband and I began our journey into research on the Internet and finally found out about the Autism Research Institute. I called Dr. Bernie Rimland, who headed the institute at the time (he passed away in 2006). He told me four words that forever changed our lives: You... can...treat...autism. He went on to tell me about all the wonderful medical treatments, like vitamins, detox, and numerous other therapies that are helping these kids get better.

I ran into Glen's office and screamed, "There's a lot we can do!" Glen got on the phone with Kirkman Laboratories and talked to DAN! doctors and started to get on board with biomedical intervention. We were on our way!

At this point in my life I got so excited because I knew deep down inside that there had to be something more than just behavior therapies. We went to our first Defeat Autism Now! conference and I was blown away by the amount of information and confidence these doctors had in treating children with autism. We came home from the conference trying to figure out where to start.

Our first mission was to eliminate wheat and dairy. We had to pull out of his diet the only food that Jeff would eat! The first thing I did was crack the code of chicken nuggets. I must have made eight pounds of gluten- and casein-free chicken nuggets only to find that Jeff would not eat them. The problem was that Jeff would eat only Burger King chicken nuggets. So I drove to Burger King and said to the manager, "Listen, I'm gonna give you ten bucks and I want twenty empty little boxes and bags." He saw the desperation in my eyes and handed me the goods without the need of cash. I was trying to trick my son into thinking these new healthy nuggets came from Burger King, but I didn't care.

At home, I put the chicken nuggets inside the Burger King box and told Jeff, "Mommy's going to get nuggets!" Then I went outside and walked once around my car (Jeff had no concept of time). I walked back in the door, holding the Burger King bag victoriously. I remember walking to the table, handing the bag to him, and holding my breath. It was the moment of truth. Could I possibly trick a child who ate chicken nuggets only from Burger King into thinking these GFCF ones I'd made were the same? He tore the box open and slowly moved a nugget into his mouth. He chewed and chewed and then swallowed. I was so excited. I did it! It worked.

One of the things we noticed right away after changing the diet was that the rashes slowly went away and the explosive diarrhea went down to one time a day. Jeff was still waking up a lot during the night, though. We had yet to crack the "sleep through the night" code, and as a result,

Mom and Dad were up most nights, too. This meant home and marriage life was a challenge and close to the edge of breaking...daily.

A few months later, we went to another autism conference, where I watched a doctor give a speech and said to myself, "This man is really sincere. I like him." He came down from the stage and I walked right up to him and said, "Dr. Jerry Kartzinel, I'm Lisa Ackerman. I am so excited about you! My son is going to be your patient. Isn't that great?" He looked at me oddly for a moment, like I was a stalker. I really liked this doctor and my mommy instinct said he's the one! Dr. Jerry Kartzinel gave us more things to do and I was eager to put my energy into this because dealing with any type of emotions just sucked.

My marriage was in big trouble and I had probably divorced my husband fifteen times in my head by now. Then the reality check came in and kicked me in the ass. Our then sixteen-year-old daughter came into the room and told me she really needed to talk to me. I knew it was going to be about some drama because she's sixteen and in high school. She went on to tell me how everyone sucks and yada yada yada, and I said to her, "Lauren, I don't care what your friend said. I don't care what happened at your school today. You've got that bitchy sixteen-year-old look on your face about some friend telling you something that hurt your feelings. I really don't care."

She looked at me for a moment and started crying. Then she said, "You know, you have TWO kids, Mom."

My world stopped. This is the other moment in my life

where I died. I had been so bad with Lauren. I would even write her checks to manage her own life because I couldn't. I had nothing for anyone but Jeff. I had become this single-focused person whom no one wanted to live with. Even I didn't want to live with me. I tried to think back to the time when I was a nurturing person. That is who I wanted to be again.

I apologized to Lauren. I was so grateful to her for being the one to turn my emotions back on.

I walked into my bedroom and looked at Glen and said, "I'm sorry. I'm the biggest dick in the whole world."

"So am I," he said.

We hugged each other. We still fought over the dumbest things, like leaving shoes in the wrong place, but we still had one really good thing in common: We both wanted Jeff to get better and loved talking about new treatments we found.

At this point Jeff still wasn't speaking and he was addicted to collecting Snapple lids. He was also really into Carmex lip balms and candy bars. He didn't eat the candy bars; he just had to have one in each hand in order to walk. These strange objects were almost like periods at the end of a sentence. Whenever we traveled, it was with forty-eight Snapple lids and twelve things of Carmex, and we'd hit stores for candy bars all the time.

After getting Jeff's test results back, Dr. Kartzinel told us that he had strange parasites, almost forty times more yeast than normal, and a number of other things. So we started Jeff on antifungals to get rid of yeast. He didn't have a hard die-off period when he went crazy like most moms describe. He was mellow.

The first change in Jeff I noticed was when he was sitting down one night and started looking at a book. I stood there shocked because usually the book would be used to hit someone in the head. Now he was actually looking at the book. He was looking at it so intently that I leaned down and pointed to the picture of the dog and said "woof woof," and then I chewed on him and he giggled. He giggled!

Jeff loved being with his ABA therapists, and I must say ABA made a huge difference in helping Jeff. But he had so many health issues that we had to keep pounding the dirt with biomedical treatments while also trusting ABA to do its thing. Our boy was physically sick and that's what we were focused on.

Our next plan of action was chelation (detoxing metals in the body). I was scared to try it at first, so I made sure I thoroughly researched it before we did it. Through extensive research and dozens of calls to pharmaceutical companies, I found out that Jeff had received at least 125 micrograms of mercury through thimerosal, the preservative in the vaccines injected into him. This made me sick to my stomach. I got really drunk at home and I remember thinking, "I'm like Arthur," that drunk from the movie of the same name.

I drank because I knew the autism was probably preventable. I didn't think, "Hey, something or someone totally destroyed my child." I just thought of it all on a massive scale, how many people this was happening to and how many more people were going to have to learn the hard way, like me. I was scared thinking how global this was and how it was only going to get worse unless people woke up. I was scared.

Jeff would need to be a four-hundred-pound man to assimilate the 125 micrograms of mercury he received from the vaccines. (There are actually no safety studies on mercury exposure for children.) So I thought to myself, "Do I keep this shit in there and continue to let it do damage?" The way I looked at it, it was eating his soul every day, eating his organs. I realized it's worse for it to be in there and decided to try to get the bad stuff out.

With Dr. Kartzinel's help, we went through a number of chelators, but they all gave Jeff a huge yeast problem, so we had to take him off. We decided to go the supplementation route and found glutathione. If you can restore glutathione levels in the body, the body will naturally detoxify some of the metals. That's what glutathione does! We did this by going through a five-minute IV push of glutathione. This involved Glen using all of his Herculean strength to pin Jeff down in a bobsled hold while I danced around the room with a DVD player.

I kept wiping his tears away, saying, "This is going to help him, this is going to help him, this is going to help him." We eventually restored Jeff's glutathione levels and got his complexion back. The dark circles under his eyes got better. Finally at this point Jeff started to sleep better, act better. He was beginning to copy our talking.

There had been so much screaming through the years.

Now, hearing him laugh is what kept me going. Just a laugh here and there. It was my medicine.

We now moved from a PECS (Picture Exchange Communication System) strategy for communication and acquired an augmentative communication device so Jeff could point to words. This device was the coolest thing. Jeff would press buttons on the machine that would say things like "I...want...cookie..." and the amazing thing was that he started to imitate the machine and actually say "I want cookie." He had very severe apraxia (inability to move his mouth muscles) so he was still not intelligible to most people, but he was trying. Nine months after we got that device, we got rid of it because Jeff started to talk. He was five years old now and not only did he start talking, he started singing! I would go into the shower and cry my eyes out because my boy was singing a Winnie the Pooh song.

I still had plenty of rage at this time. It wasn't all songs and smiles. I was angry. There is a scene in the movie *The Princess Bride* in which the character says, "My name is Inigo Montoya. You killed my father, prepare to die." Well, my name is Lisa Ackerman, you poisoned my kid, and I want those years back. He deserves those lost years. I have a lot of anger about that.

By the time we got Jeff into his second round of kindergarten at a mainstream school, we got him a FM auditory trainer hearing aid because his hearing was so sensitive. The sound of someone talking or walking outside the classroom would be the same decibel as the teacher talking. This hearing device allowed the teacher's voice to go straight into my son's ear, and he began to do some things on his own in class with no aid.

One thing I always tell people to do is to NOT hang on to a security blanket. Raise the bar constantly. I found that every time we raised the bar for Jeff, he always rose to meet it. If something did not work, we got creative and figured out an alternative approach. Yeah, he still needed aid in school, he still needed help, but he would always rise to the occasion. Some people told me that my son could only be in special education classes. They tried hard to push Jeff into those classes, but by the second round of kindergarten, he was in a typical class. And to this day I am so grateful because he is still in a mainstream education setting. How will our kids be part of society if other kids don't know what they are dealing with? By placing Jeff in a mainstream setting with the right support, something great happened. A boy named Jeff benefited. Autism helped the teacher. It helped all the kids in the class. For our family and for Jeff—this strategy worked.

During the summer of second grade, we started to do mild hyperbaric oxygen therapy. Jeff was prescribed for forty sessions and I was annoyed at first going to these sessions because I felt they were eating up time in our day. It was taking away from speech therapy and I began to get irritated. I would call Glen and whine, "This sucks, sucks, sucks, sucks, sucks!" Then, on the twenty-first session, we came out of the tank, and the chamber dude, Eddie, looked at Jeff and asked, "How do you feel?"

Jeff looked at him and said, "I'm good, Eddie, how are you?"

Eddie said, "Do you want to come back tomorrow?"

"Yeah, come back tomorrow."

"What are you going to do now, Jeff?"

"I go home."

"What are you going to do at home?"

"Time to eat dinner."

And I started freaking out but trying to act cool at the same time and said, "What do you want for dinner, Jeff?"

"Can I have a turkey burger, Mom?"

"Yes, and what do you want for dessert?"

"Cookies!"

"What do you want to do after cookies, Jeff?"

"Movie!"

I called Glen on the way home, screaming, "Hyperbaric therapy is the best thing in the world! I love it!"

We had to make sure, though, and I want to tell parents to make sure your children have their antioxidants and their amino acids in check so they don't go into oxidative stress.

Jeff still had good days and bad days. And when Jeff had a bad day, I had a bad day, and when Jeff had a good day everyone had a good day.

Six years into treating Jeff medically and with traditional therapies, he suddenly stopped pooping. I freaked out. What's going on now, what happened? There was a major change in his sleep patterns and he had a distended belly. After reviewing his X-ray Dr. Kartzinel insisted that we do an endoscopy.

After the procedure, the doctor concluded Jeff had erosion in his esophagus from recurring reflux, and a polyp in his esophagus base. The reflux finally explained why he didn't sleep well. My son could tell me what he wanted for dinner but he could not tell me his stomach hurt, and the pain from the reflux was huge. The doctor then told us he had ileitis, which is the precursor to colitis. He also has lymphoid nodular hyperplasia—a medical condition that does not exist in any other member of our family. I asked the doctor if this looked like what he saw with other vaccine-injured kids with autism and he said yes.

I immediately flashed back to that MMR and I became ill. That's when Jeff had fallen apart. Right after that MMR shot. It all made sense. We started Jeff on medication for both the inflammation and the reflux. His doctor was pleased that Jeff had already been on the gluten- and casein-free and allergen-free diet for six years. Jeff's gastroenterologist prescribed anti-inflammatories and reflux medication, which greatly improved the poop and sleep situations. The side benefit from this treatment plan was that Jeff continued to improve in school and at home.

At seven years of age and after more medical tests, Jeff was prescribed Valtrex by Dr. Kartzinel. Two months later, Jeff started using adjectives. Then we added L-carnitine supplements and noticed more subtle differences.

Jeff is in fourth grade now and is in mainstream classrooms with an aide. He's great with his friends, takes turns, jokes, and asks to play with them. He is not recovered, but he wins the award for biggest comeback. I believe my son is a walking miracle and there are so many amazing things about him, and that is what I focus on.

I began a support group in my living room with only ten parents sitting on my floor and we gave each other action items to do or try out. I call these people "the first ten" because ten people quickly turned into sixty people and soon after that, my neighbors started complaining that the street was crowded with cars! I said, "We gotta move this someplace else and give ourselves a name." The Lisa Ackerman Diet Support Group was no longer an appropriate name because of the massive growth and all that we were doing to build community and help our kids. So we moved and called ourselves TACA, for Talk About Curing Autism. We moved to a church and today I'm proud to say TACA has seven thousand members and fifteen chapters across the country. Strength in numbers, right? We will continue to bring education and support so parents can bring it forward, whether it's recovery or getting our kids to be the best they can be. That's what we are all about.

My name is Lisa Ackerman. Autism is treatable. Prepare to recover!

TACA CAN HELP YOU get the information you need to best help your child and change your child's future. Visit talkaboutcuringautism.org.

15

Siblings

LISA'S STORY MADE ME realize that no one ever talks about the siblings. There is a whole generation that people lose sight of and it is these children, the siblings. When a child in the home has autism, all the attention goes toward that child. Naturally, the focus is to help heal him or her. There are endless therapists who come in to work with the child, and from the sibling's point of view, it can look as if the therapists are playing with the child, leaving the sibling to wonder why he or she is being ignored. The sibling will often seek attention from Mom, but when all of Mom's attention and energy is on the other child, the sibling will usually look elsewhere. Perhaps they look to Dad, but many of the dads are not there, either divorced or always putting in extra hours at work. What are siblings left to do? They become embarrassed to have their friends over because their brother is stimming or acting weird. Some siblings are forced to eat their favorite foods in the garage because it's not gluten- or casein-free. I know some families that purposely had another child so he or she could take care of the one with autism long after the parents are dead. This is a huge problem. The sibling generation should not be ignored or overlooked or used in any way. Nurture them, respect them, and listen to them.

These children are the ones who will be changing the world to help children with autism. They are the ones who will be left with the responsibility long after we're gone. They are the hand that will be holding our kids' hands and leading them into a bright future. Let's start to give them the respect they deserve, too.

16

What a "Trip"

I WAS SITTING in an airport recently, watching a little boy, about the age of ten, scream and flap his arms while running around in circles. People all around the terminal were staring at him and shaking their heads, looking disgusted. The woman next to me leaned over to her friend and said, "Geez, can't that lady control her kid?" My heart sank as I watched this mom chase her uncontrollable screaming child through the airport while getting dirty looks from people. She pulled toy after toy out of her bag, hoping that one toy might hold her child's attention, but nothing would calm him down. It was obvious to me that it was autism, but to all the people in the terminal, he just looked like an obnoxious, misbehaving boy.

The woman next to me kept whispering to herself, "Shut up, you little brat." I could feel my blood pressure rising and was ready to explode on her with the next comment she made. "Is it take-your-spoiled-brat-to-the-airport-day?" the woman said.

I leaned over and firmly said, "That child has autism, he's not a brat. He can't control his behavior and you shouldn't be judging that mother."

The woman replied, "How can you tell it's autism? He just looks like a screaming brat."

As I gave her my lecture on autism and told her about some of the signs like flapping of the hands and other stims, or repetitive motions, I began to think about how these kids don't have physical characteristcs that make them look unique. Down syndrome has a particular look that makes it easier for people to identify. Autism looks like a spoiled child being raised by a mother who has no control.

After I finished telling off the woman sitting next to me, I went online to see if I could find anything interesting about raising a child with special needs. I wondered what might be out there on the Web or if there was anything inspirational, and I'm very glad I looked because I would have missed out on this beautiful trip to Holland:

WELCOME TO HOLLAND
by Emily Perl Kingsley

I am often asked to describe the experience of rais-ing a child with a disability—to try to help people who have not shared that unique experience to under-stand it, to imagine how it would feel. It's like this....

When you're going to have a baby, it's like planning a fabulous trip to Italy. You buy a bunch of guidebooks and make your wonderful plans. The Coliseum. Michelangelo's David. The gondolas in Venice. You may learn some handy phrases in Italian. It's all very exciting. After months of eager anticipation, the day finally arrives. You pack your bags and off you go. Several hours later, the plane lands. The stewardess comes in and says, "Welcome to Holland."

"Holland?!?" you say. "What do you mean Holland?? I signed up for Italy! I'm supposed to be in Italy. All my life I've dreamed of going to Italy."

But there's been a change in the flight plan. They've landed in Holland and there you must stay. The important thing is that they haven't taken you to a horrible, disgusting, filthy place, full of pestilence, famine, and disease. It's just a different place. So you must go out and buy new guidebooks. And you must learn a whole new language. And you will meet a whole new group of people you would never have met. It's just a *different* place. It's slower-paced than Italy, less flashy than Italy. But after you've been there for a while and you catch your breath, you look around...and you begin to notice that Holland has windmills...and Holland has tulips. Holland even has Rembrandts. But everyone you know is busy coming and going from Italy...and they're all bragging about what a wonderful time they had there. And for the rest of your life, you will say, "Yes, that's where I was supposed to go. That's what I had planned." And the pain of that will never, ever, ever, ever go away...because the loss of that dream is a very, very significant loss. But if you spend your life mourning the fact that you didn't get to Italy, you may never be free to enjoy the very special, the very lovely things...about Holland.

17

Becky Behnan:
Mother Warrior to Jack

YOU'RE NEVER TOO OLD

People occasionally say to me, "Jenny, you never talk about the older kids with autism, the ones who came before the epidemic." My phone rang late one afternoon and it was a sixty-year-old woman who had a thirty-year-old son with autism still living with her. I was captivated by her story and couldn't wait to get on a plane to fly to Las Vegas to interview her. Later on, I would learn that she was the daughter of one of the first well-known casino owners in Las Vegas back in the day. Kind of like a Clint Eastwood cowboy meets *GoodFellas*. But walking into the interview, all I knew was that she was a warrior who paved the way for us, and that we could all learn from her experiences.

"YOUR SON IS AUTISTIC." It was 1979 when the doctor told me Jack had autism. Ironically, my husband and I had remembered reading this article about a child with autism who had strange behaviors and how the mother would control her son with a picture of Alfred Hitchcock. She said that it was the only way to control her son because the child was scared to death of Alfred Hitchcock. We found it very strange and fascinating. Many years later, when we received the same diagnosis for our son, Jack, my husband and I were completely devastated, to say the least. Then, soon after my son's diagnosis, my sister shot herself in the face. She was attempting suicide and did not succeed—until a few years later. My journey has been a difficult one, but I have surprised many people with how I carried on.

When I hear parents today talk about how they don't know which direction to go after hearing their child's diagnosis, I say, "Can you even imagine how difficult it was in 1979?" No one knew what autism was and my husband and I really had no idea ourselves except for the Alfred Hitchcock story. But we knew one thing for sure: Autism was a bad situation. So my husband and I had a plan, not a very good one, but it seemed good at the time. We decided to fight this label they gave Jack and went from doctor to doctor hoping to find one doctor who would say, "They were wrong, this isn't autism, everything's going to be fine." Needless to say, we couldn't find a doctor who disagreed with the original diagnosis. In fact, we couldn't find many doctors who knew about autism. They all had to look it up.

One doctor said Jack could just be deaf so I got on the

phone with Dr. John House of the House Ear Institute and he told me to get to Los Angeles as soon as possible. I flew right over to the institute and they asked me to try to put Jack to sleep to enable them to test his hearing because he was so unruly. I knew he wouldn't go to sleep and knew the only way to get him to sleep was to drive around in a car. So I took Jack outside and jumped into a cab. Just my luck, too, the cab driver was dressed in full drag. This was Hollywood, so I wasn't too surprised. The driver was incredibly nice. I talked about my plight, and the driver just drove around, swaying the car back and forth until Jack fell asleep. When I finally got back to the hospital, the doctor had left. He had seen me get into the cab and thought I had gone for the day. I was forced to go buy diapers and spend the night in Hollywood. The next day they tested his hearing and said Jack was fine. He had no hearing problems at all.

LISTENING TO BECKY talk about Jack's hearing test made me reflect on Evan's first hearing test. I remember being in the waiting room hoping that Evan was deaf, not autistic. I was envisioning him getting an implant in his ear so he could hear us and respond again. That to me seemed like an easier fix because autism scared the living hell out of me. So many parents I talk to have gone through this same hearing test to rule out deafness. I know our children stop responding to their names, but if you throw on a Baby Einstein DVD loudly in another room, I would bet millions of dollars your child would run in there to listen to the beautiful "music"

that moves them. It's a really good basic hearing test to try at home.

I DIDN'T KNOW WHAT to do next, so I listened to my motherly instinct and it told me to keep Jack around typical children as much as possible. Every doctor at this point kept saying to me, "no known cause, no known cure." And at every big place I went to, like UCLA, they didn't know anything. It was only 1979. Not only was there no hope yet but people still hadn't a clue as to what to do with it. And I'll never forget what one doctor said to me: "You'll always think it's gonna get better...but it never will." I wish he had never said that to me. It's been really hard to let it go. I wish he had offered at least a little hope.

IT'S TRUE WHAT Becky says about hope. The medical community needs to offer some hope no matter what the diagnosis. I don't care if it's a terminal illness, no one should ever say there is nothing you can do. Miracles can happen, faith can move mountains, and doctors need to learn about a medicine called Hope.

WITHIN MY HOUSE, chaos had set in. My husband was having a really hard time with Jack's diagnosis. He was supportive but carried a lot of pain with him. The only good thing about the beginning stages of autism for Jack was that the tantrums had not yet started. Well, they were starting, but they weren't bad yet. I kept trying to talk to as many people as I could to see if they knew of anyone who could help me. My father, being the kind of guy nobody dared to mess with out here in Vegas, had many connections and opened doors for me and gave me money to help Jack. But the science to heal autism was not up to par yet, so all the money and all the connections in the world couldn't push medicine fast enough.

Every place I continued to search for help, like the top-notch hospitals in Houston and at UCLA, still knew nothing. Then someone finally mentioned to me a doctor by the name of Bernie Rimland. (Dr. Bernie Rimland was the founder of Autism Research Institute and passed on in 2006. He was one of the first doctors, in the 1960s, to go out to the media and say that autism can be caused by environmental toxins and that diet, detox, and supplements can alleviate symptoms of autism. If only we had listened to him back then, how different things might have been.)

Bernie told me about a place in Florida that was run by a Dr. William Philpott. He was working on curing schizophrenia. Back then, they called autism "childhood schizophrenia" more than they called it autism.

I went down to his place in St. Petersburg, Florida, and I must have stayed there for two months or something, at the clinic with the schizophrenics. I had hoped this was not what I was facing, because it was grim. It was pretty hard seeing schizophrenic people. They were getting shock treatment. I wasn't going to give up, though. I knew if I couldn't figure this out, I might not be able to keep Jack. Doctors along the way had told me Jack would have to be in an institution. Some wanted me to institutionalize him from the beginning. But the only institution for Jack would be my home. I would put a gate around it if I had to. In fact, we did put a gate around it.

It's scary to think that some of these children are going to need to be institutionalized and there aren't going to be any institutions to put them in. And the government is not going to do anything about it, because they didn't do anything for schizophrenic homeless people. We see so many schizophrenic homeless people and it saddens me to know that someday they are going to be joined by autistic adults if we don't do something about it.

I loved Dr. Philpott because he was able to think outside the box. As soon as we got there, he tested Jack's biochemical breakdown. He checked for metals and lead, and he told me to take him off of wheat. He talked to me about amino acids and candida, which I think is a huge, huge thing now. When I read about it in *Louder Than Words*, I said, "Oh my God." It was the first time I'd heard "candida" in a long, long time, and that doctor told me about all this stuff back in the 1970s! Everything the doctor did to my son, I made sure he did to me, too. Jack got an IV drip; so did I. Jack took certain things; so did I. We were a team.

I heard about Dr. Lovaas, who was starting to implement treatment on kids with autism, so I flew down to see him. He was so depressing. He used to force the children to smell ammonia. There was no way I was leaving my son with Lovaas. During that time, they were still doing this to autistic kids. They don't do it anymore. They just reward kids with candy treats they shouldn't have. Lovaas had gone on to tell me that my marriage was going to fail, and that it was going to ruin my other son and the best thing I could do for the whole family was to put Jack in an institution. So that's when I came home, and my father moved in to help. There was just no way I was going to let Lovaas's predictions happen.

So we were continuing to follow Dr. Philpott's protocol, even though it was way out there. We did something called ozone therapy, involving ozone, oxygen, and hydrogen peroxide. We got our ozone machine, and we didn't even know what we were doing. The instructions were in German; the Germans deal with this all the time. They work with ozone constantly. It's an incredible cure. We can't breathe it, but we could inject it. And it was really scary. We tried some, and then my dad's nurse tried it. She was a black nurse and when she took a shot of it, she turned white, right there where the shot hit. She turned white. So we didn't know what we were doing, but we were that desperate to keep searching.

Time had gone by and Lovaas had come out with the beginnings of a behavioral therapy. Two men then came to my house to teach me the technique, but the technique was to scream at the child; I have it on tape. If the kid did something wrong, you were supposed to scream as loud as you could in his face, "NO!" This was approximately 1981. They were still figuring things out and so was I.

The most important thing that happened in our life was a woman named Anne McGinnis. She moved in with us for a few months and my father took my older son away for this period of time because Anne said, "We're going to have to do these pin-downs with your son." Because Jack had no eye contact, he was like a wild whirlwind that ran through the house. She started putting tape around her wrists as if we were going to war or something. And she said, "Well, it's gonna be quite an endeavor here." So the first pin-down we had, we held him down for eight hours. We'd have to take shifts because he fought us the whole time. I've been around a ranch before and it was like breaking a horse. The first one was eight hours, the next one was six hours, and the next one was a little less.

We were hoping the treatment would make Jack attend to us, pay attention to us, because he didn't want to stop doing what he wanted to do. It was like the part in *Louder Than Words* when Evan screams all day. Jack just did what he wanted. He'd go all over the place and not look at anyone. It was an impossible situation. Jack was out of control.

After a few months with Anne, the treatments started to work. I'll be darned if Jack didn't start making some eye contact. And of course the minute we got any eye contact, we would say "good looking" or "good sitting," and she got his behaviors under control. It's amazing that it worked.

Of course it was terrible to hold him down and listen to that screaming. But you know what? Just before the treatment, he would grab me by my hair and throw me all over. And he was just a little kid. And I thought, "Well, if I don't get these behaviors under control now, I'm in trouble. He's gonna get big."

I WAS AMAZED to listen to Becky talk about the therapies from over twenty years ago. This first group of kids had to endure so much more pain because science was experimenting on them to figure out what worked and what didn't. I pictured Becky pinning her son down for eight hours a day and all I could think was, "Wow, these are the real heroes. The generation of autism that Becky lived through pioneered it for all of us."

YOU KNOW WHAT got me through it all? Right outside my window, across the street, there is a house. That family's son had been kidnapped. When I would get depressed, I'd look out that window and say, "Oh, I don't have a problem. I know where my child is." That is what got me through it, those people across the street. The little boy never did show up, never did come back. The parents divorced, and she left with the other kids and he stayed there until just five years ago. I think he was always hoping that someone had his son and that he'd get away or come back. The dad finally gave up and moved. They are what gave me strength.

I never really met anyone else who had kids on the autism spectrum. When I did, I would invite them to my house to listen to doctors I'd have come over. And I'll never forget there was a woman who came and her little boy was autistic, and he had this bandage on his hand. I asked the lady, "What happened to your son?"

"He shot himself. He found a gun and he shot himself."

And she was just so nonchalant about it. It was like she really wanted him to find that gun and kill himself. This is what I felt. I knew this woman wanted her child to not be around anymore. He didn't know anyone existed and would just walk right through you. One time I was trying to control him while she was talking to a doctor, and I couldn't. He was about ten years old and there was no way I could control him. He was big. It was so sad.

Jack had echolalia. He echoed everything you'd say. "Hi, Jack," I'd say and he would reply, "Hi, Jack." Finally we found a therapist who used the Peabody Language Development Kits, which had puppets. I had a maid's quarters outside and we turned that into a classroom and she worked with Jack every day. She was another person who came into my life and made a difference. Her name was Peggy. She'd sit out there all day with him and make him practice language and do exercises with him and use the puppets.

He didn't have meaningful language until he was eight years old. And we fought hard to get him into schools that rejected him, even special ed schools. By the time high school came, we put him in a mainstream school, but he was beaten up so many times by mean jocks. The kids really made fun of him.

When Jack turned twenty, we decided to teach him how to be a card dealer. I wanted him to have a job and because we owned a casino, we knew we could protect him and watch over him. So we had him train with an expert dealer and he did great.

By the time he was done training, he could deal 21, roulette, craps, and baccarat. And he loved learning it. We thought we had taught him everything there is to know about dealing, but on his first day on the job, a cocktail waitress came to the table where he was dealing roulette and asked if anyone wanted drinks. Jack raised his hand and said, "I'll take a 7up," not really understanding that the waitress was talking to the customers, not to him. He was totally uninhibited and still is. In fact, when the casino had to take the required fingerprint and mug shot of the dealers, he kept yelling, "I'm innocent, but I'm innocent!" He takes things literally.

Unfortunately, not too long after he started working, Jack had a regression. He took many steps backward because my brother was murdered. After Jack found out, the regression happened because his anger was out of control. He was deeply upset that his uncle was murdered. He broke a few car windshields with his bare fists in outbursts of anger. He is so much better now. He doesn't get that angry anymore, but it was amazing to watch him try to deal with that kind of emotional pain.

DURING MY INTERVIEW with Becky, the front door opened and Jack came walking through the door. I couldn't wait to meet him, so I jumped out of my seat. He is a handsome thirty-year-old man with a smile better than most movie stars. He began to tell me about how he knows who I am because he saw me on E! Entertainment news. He said that he knew I was dating Jim Carrey and that he knew every movie Jim did and the year he did them. He also went on to tell me that *Liar Liar* and *Dumb and Dumber* were his favorite movies. While Jack talked, I of course observed his behavior to see how much autism I could see. I have to say, for a couple of minutes I had no idea. He seemed extremely polite, with a little bit of oddity in the tone of his voice. He was fully conversational and the only hiccup I might have seen was his not elaborating on or extending his thoughts.

I was taken aback by how much light was coming out of this man. I truly couldn't get enough of his energy. He was like a lightbulb that went on when he walked into the room. He asked me if I could answer one question before he went out again. I said, "Of course, Jack. What is it?"

"What ever happened to Yasmine Bleeth?"

I smiled and paused for a moment. Of all the questions in the world he could have asked, he wanted to know what happened to Yasmine Bleeth, the former *Baywatch* beauty. I loved it. I told him I thought she moved back home to be with her family in Michigan. I'm not sure if I was right but I figured an answer would help him close the chapter on whatever happened to one of his favorite *Baywatch* babes.

After Jack left, I asked Becky about his social life. I wanted to know if he dates, considering he is a thirty-year-old man. "Yes, he dates. Well, he dates prostitutes. He has to pay for his dates, but he tells me sometimes he buys stuff for them like he would for a girlfriend."

I paused for a moment and asked, "Can I put this in my book?"

"Absolutely. I think it is a big breakthrough, and I think that's where a lot of people are going to have a lot of problems. They're going to be closed minded about it, and you better be very open-minded about it, because sex is a natural part of men's lives."

I was grateful Becky was being so open about this real issue of sex that the new generation of autism hasn't had to deal with yet. These men will have sexual needs someday, and the fact that they won't be socially sophisticated enough to know how to manipulate woman like typical guys do for sex makes me wonder what the hell it's gonna be like.

JACK DOESN'T KNOW he has autism. We tried to keep that label away for so long that we never told him. He knows about Evan because of what I told him and he says that he prays for him to get better. But I don't want Jack to see autism behaviors. I don't want him to think, "I'm like that?" That would really freak him out. It would do more damage than good.

Just a few nights ago he woke me up while I was in bed and asked, "What's wrong with me?" I asked him what he meant and he said he thinks like an old person. It must be that his thoughts are not coming out clearly, because my mother had dementia and he saw her and he knows it's not correct.

Despite all of this, I do believe Jack could live on his own, but it wouldn't be wise because he's still very gullible. He'd still need monitoring. But as far as being able to go to the store, buy groceries, keep himself clean, keep the room clean, whatever, yes, he could handle it. My other son, Bennie, will eventually take Jack after I'm gone. Thank God I have Bennie, because some members of my family have chosen not to have contact with Jack for years now.

Jack has a few people in his life who stayed dear to him and I bless those people every day because it takes a lot of unconditional love, patience, and understanding to be in someone's life who has autism and the few who have stuck by us I will forever be indebted to.

I talk all the time about how poignant Jim Carrey's movie *The Truman Show* is to me. We made this perfect world for Jack just like they did in *The Truman Show*. The similarities are incredible. Because my father was a casino owner, nobody was going to break any rules and mess with the perfect bubble we made for Jack. We wondered constantly, "Do we tell Jack? Are we doing right by him? Are we doing wrong by him?" Everything is controlled in his environment, just like it is for Truman. After the movie was done, I sat by myself in the theatre and cried because I had created *The Truman Show* with my own child.

I THINK MANY PARENTS can relate to Becky's analogy of *The Truman Show*. I know I can. Even though Evan is doing great, I still pick out his friends to make sure they best suit him. I make sure that everything that happens around him is under my control. When do I let go? I can see from Becky that it might be hard to ever let go. There are going to be a lot of Trumans out there. Many can hide their autism label, but Evan won't ever be able to hide from it. When people say to me, "You made Evan the poster child for autism," I reply with, "No, I made him a poster child for hope."

As I continued talking to Becky, I asked, "Many parents believe that a certain vaccination triggered their child's autism. Jack was diagnosed in 1979 when vaccinations weren't as controversial. Do you believe that Jack had any sort of reaction to a vaccine that might have triggered his autism?"

"Yes. I can even tell you what Jack was wearing the day he had the vaccination that I believe triggered his autism. I can tell you everything about that day. The doctor previously told me that Jack's immune system was going to be down because he had to have two blood transfers after he was born. My motherly instinct at the doctor's office told me that maybe he shouldn't be vaccinated because his immune system was weak. And then they said, 'Oh, no, you don't want him to catch these diseases that the vaccinations could protect him from. You really need to have these.' But my alarm was going off, saying this doesn't make sense. I didn't want them to do it and they did it anyway. I'll never forget that moment."

I WISH I COULD have stayed and talked to Becky longer, but I had to wrap up the interview to make my flight back to Los Angeles. I hugged her and thanked her immensely for her honesty and sharing her incredible journey with the world. I asked her if she had any last words for moms out there. She replied, "I have three simple words that seem impossible at times but are the most important words for parents who are on this journey called autism, and they are...

"Never...give...up."

Then she smiled at me and added, "No matter how old you are. Look at me. I'm sixty and that's not stopping me."

18

My Autism Whisperer

WITH THE DIVORCE RATE in autism families being 80 percent there are many single mothers out there going through this journey alone. So many single moms approach me and ask if they will ever find someone like I did who would be open and willing to fall in love with them and their autistic child. Many men have a hard time getting into relationships with women who have typical children, let alone autistic children. So I decided to sit down with Jim right before bed one night and ask him to share his thoughts and feelings about our relationship and about Evan.

I plopped my head on a pillow and stared at his beautiful, sweet face as he began to open up his heart.

IN THE BEGINNING of our relationship we were just dating so I wasn't thinking too much about taking on any roles of a family unit quite yet. But I was always interested in what you had to say about Evan and about the things you had to overcome and deal with as far as autism was concerned. As time went on, I fell in love with your strength and good humor in the midst of all that.

The first time I met Evan, he was just this little ball of light. He didn't say much and it was hard in the beginning because there was no back-and-forth conversation with him. Usually, as you get to know someone, they open up and want hugs and affection, but because he had autism, there was always a little bit of distance. It was difficult not to take it personally when he seemed to be ignoring my attention.

I just had to be patient and give him enough love and attention, and soon I became the interesting thing in the room to him. Now we're buds. He trusts me.

I fell in love with you and knew that if we were meant to be together for the rest of our lives, then that meant Evan was supposed to be there, too. I made the commitment to love you both, and decided that all of it was going to be a blessing.

Before you both moved in, I had to seriously consider the responsibility of helping raise Evan, but once I let go of the fear and decided to love him, our life together became really fun. I soon realized that I was going to learn as much from Evan as he was from me. I've gained the capacity for love, acceptance, and patience, and the ability to make someone feel safe. Last night Evan was frightened so he crawled into bed with us and went to sleep. By four A.M., he had turned his whole body sideways and began kicking me in the face over and over. But instead of moving him, I just lay there laughing and taking the blows. I had to get up at six A.M. the next morning and shoot for twelve hours, but moments like that have become much more valuable to me than a good night's sleep. I just love it.

We have many things in common, Jenny and I, not the least of which is our love for a beautiful little boy named Evan. A little boy whose terrible struggle cracked open her heart and revealed to me a depth of character and spirit that is undeniably pure. It was Evan who made me understand her true worth. That's just one little thing he's done for us.

For single moms out there struggling with autism and looking for love, you have to change the belief that you'll never meet a guy who will take it all on, because whatever you believe will become your reality. If you believe no one can love you, it will be difficult, if not impossible, to attract

Photographed by Tracey Landworth at an Exceptional Events production.

someone. Believe that there are good men out there who will love you and your child, and you will attract one of them. The universe is listening and creating your life based on what you believe. So don't send out the wrong signals. Convince yourself that you deserve love and it will happen.

19

Katie Wright: Mother Warrior to Christian

IN CASE PEOPLE DON'T KNOW who Katie Wright is, I'll fill you in. I'm sure you've heard of Autism Speaks, the largest autism organization in the country. Autism Speaks seems to have a presence at every event, and it seems as though every rich person in the world donates to the organization. To the rest of the country, they might seem to have their hearts and minds in the right place, but many of us who have kids with autism aren't as pleased with Autism Speaks.

When I pulled back the curtain on Autism Speaks, I was shocked that this organization does not stand behind those who believe in biomedical treatment for autism. I was surprised to find that most of their research money goes toward genetics, and nothing goes toward researching environmental components that could trigger autism in kids who have genetic vulnerabilities. I was surprised that the first time I went on the Autism Speaks Web site, there was no reference to the gluten-free, casein-free diet. I was surprised there was no mention of DAN! doctors.

I was initially moved by the story of why Autism Speaks was founded in the first place. Suzanne and Bob Wright (a former NBC exec) founded Autism Speaks because their grandson Christian Hildebrand was diagnosed with autism and they wanted to get some national help and attention for the cause. I remember feeling so disappointed when I discovered that this huge organization was ignoring the screams and yells of parents who had actually found treatments to help our children. I remember thinking, "I wonder what the daughter of Bob and Suzanne thinks about all this? Does she agree with her parents? Does she know that there is a large part of the autism community that doesn't support Autism Speaks? Does she even know that biomedical treatments are out there? Does she secretly believe that vaccines triggered her son's autism but is too afraid to speak up because of the empire her parents created?" I wondered if she would ever step forward and speak.

And then it happened. I was surfing the Web and read the headline that Katie Wright, daughter of Bob and Suzanne Wright, had publicly stated that she believed her son's autism was triggered by vaccines and that biomedical treatment was indeed working on her child. My mouth fell to the floor and I jumped up and down on the couch, rejoicing that she had spoken up. People thought it took courage for me to speak out, but it took tons more for Katie Wright to speak her truth when she was up against a swarm of politics and family drama. When I started writing this book, I knew that Katie would be the first Mother Warrior on my list to interview.

WHEN CHRISTIAN WAS DIAGNOSED, we were trying to figure out what to do. We tried everything: traditional therapies, ABA, speech, OT, everything. We even tried the heavy pharmaceuticals and we were warned over and over again not to do the diet, that it was very dangerous. And I, like a fool, believed them. We went to doctors all over the country, in Cleveland, Philadelphia, Boston, New York. It was a horrible time because Christian was looking horrible. Just horrible. He had dark circles under his eyes and he was gaunt. He was eating only yogurt, and then eating nothing for days.

So I thought, "You know, they keep telling me that the diet is dangerous, but what could be more dangerous than this? He's malnourished and he looks terrible." So I tried the GFCF diet and it was really hard for two days. And then he got much better. He looked better. His skin was better. I felt horrible because I had wasted so much time traveling all over the country trying antianxiety and anticonvulsant drugs on my child when I should have tried just changing his diet.

I decided to go onto the Generation Rescue Web site and contact a rescue angel. It was something like three in the morning and I was thinking, "Can somebody help me? I need direction. I don't know what to do." Then my rescue angel said, "You should try the Specific Carbohydrate Diet. Parents are seeing amazing results." So I read the book

Breaking the Vicious Cycle and learned about the Specific Carbohydrate Diet. When I asked our pediatrician about it, he said the same thing as before: "That's nuts, that's dangerous." So I decided to ignore him again and follow my hunch.

I put Christian on the Specific Carbohydrate Diet and that made the biggest difference by far. The diarrhea decreased. It went from ten horrible bowel movements a day to five, and now we're down to three and four. Also his skin and hair were so much better. Before, his hair was like sheep's fur. It was horrible. And parts of it were coming out. Parts of it were white. Also, the waking up and screaming in the middle of the night got a lot better. The biggest improvement was that the totally zoned-out look on his face was finally gone. I could see him. Before, when I would walk into the room, he wouldn't recognize me. Now he would recognize me and I would see him struggling to communicate. He was healthier and finally available for learning. I was very angry that every doctor had told me not to do the diet. And like an idiot, I listened to them for so long. When I implemented these things and they really helped, I said to myself, "I've got to speak up." And that's what made me finally want to speak out. I'm a pretty private person. I was probably the only one in my family not involved in any way at NBC. But it seemed as if a lot of people were speaking for Christian and that really bothered me.

In the beginning it was wonderful because Autism Speaks was raising awareness, which is always a good thing, but I wanted to pull my hair out when I started to see certain statements from the scientists who were running it and the people on the grant advisory board saying, "There's no connection between the gut and autism" and then questioning whether regressive autism even existed. I thought, "Come live in my house for five minutes." And so that's when I said, "That's it! I'm taking the hinges off the door! I'm going to say something now."

I felt they were using my son, using his image, using his suffering. And the pain when you go to these waiting rooms and you see the kids... it's agony.

We're living in a nightmare of autism and then to be told over and over again, "You're crazy, that's NOT what happened in YOUR house." It's more than a human being can take. I couldn't take it! I still can't take it.

I think the people, the NAAR people (National Alliance for Autism Research) at Autism Speaks, they're more old-school, more conservative. They think autism is genetic. There are people at NAAR who don't believe that there's a real environmental component at all. They think you're born like this, which makes me insane because when you have a child who's diagnosed, and you meet mom after mom with the same story as yours, it's so very frustrating!

Then one day I was on *Imus in the Morning*. The PR department at Autism Speaks really wanted me to talk about the Ad Council campaign, which was very nice, and they wanted me to talk about a lot of publicity initiatives. But I didn't feel that was my role. I wanted to speak for the moms. And Imus came right out and asked, "Do you think vaccines caused your son's autism?" I could see the PR woman from Autism Speaks was freaking out. She didn't see it, but I had brought my son's vaccine schedule book with me.

"Yes, I do. Too many shots were given too soon. I am not anti-vaccine but I believe we need a safer schedule." And I kept going and going. My dad was sitting there with me. He was surprised but he was very supportive.

When it was over, I asked my dad if he was okay with what I did. And he said, "Yeah, it's fine. It's all true. It's about what happened to you." And then the PR person at Autism Speaks came up to me and was not happy. Not happy at all! The look on her face was anger. When we got into the car, I called my mom and she told me that she got a call from someone at Autism Speaks Awareness, who was bawling, hysterically crying, saying that I was blaming mothers and that I was in with the vaccine crazies. That I was going to wreck everything.

At this point, my parents were very suspicious about the vaccine implications. I think it was awfully hard for them. I don't think they wanted it to be true. None of us wanted it to be true, but when you look at my vaccine book and see shots and fevers and regression it becomes crystal clear. My dad is a cancer survivor and in his case, the doctors really came through for him. He went the traditional route and it saved his life, so he felt that we needed to trust the doctors. But I had done that and look where it got Christian. Nowhere good. My mom was on the fence. It was very hard for them because they were getting enormous pressure from doctors and parents. I hate fighting with parents more than anything in the world, but after I was on *Imus*, my dad received hundreds of complaints about me in his office. Hundreds!

It's the researchers and scientists at Autism Speaks who won't support biomedical research. They make a great little niche for themselves. They get tons of money to do eye gazing and brain mapping. And they like it because it's not controversial and it's safe, and everybody loves them for it. It's like a little club.

I kept saying to my dad, "If this was the private sector, they'd be out of there. They've achieved nothing. They've spent hundreds of millions and done nothing. Where are the results?"

It's heartbreaking to think about the money they spent and how it could have been spent on other things. The money that was raised to go to brain mapping should have been spent on people who have an income under $35,000.

My parents, unfortunately, can't control who's on the board. They don't have the power to bring in scientists who believe in the gut-brain connection so that the board at Autism Speaks would be balanced. It's in the contract that the scientists have the power. It's been very frustrating. I have urged a number of biomedical doctors to submit grants, and they were all rejected. Arrgh! And the reason they were rejected was that apparently they didn't meet the criteria. I knew they were bullshitting me. This was political. They didn't want to fund this stuff.

Everywhere we go, moms are NOT saying we need more gene research! They're saying we need more research into the leaky gut and the rashes and the crazy allergies and all the food stuff. That's what we need help doing. It's sad, because science is too slow and scientists never spend any time with the parents. They spend their whole careers just doing gene study and eye gazing and someday they are going to realize that they missed the mark.

I believe Autism Speaks is trying to mandate insurance reimbursement for all ABA, OT, and speech therapies, which I'm proud of. The insurance companies don't want to pay for this. It's just about greed. All these therapies are scientifically proven. You can say what you want about the chelation therapy that I do with Christian, but ABA, OT, and speech are proven effective. Insurance companies just weasel out of it, and families have to pay out of pocket, which is just crazy. So my dad has been testifying in the fifty states. I think they've been in Massachusetts, Pennsylvania, Georgia—they've been all over. My parents and I have really come to a good place now where the differences I have are with Autism Speaks and not with them personally. They support my speaking out and doing what I need to do.

For a lot of children on the autism spectrum, you can't count on traditional therapies like ABA until you address the biomedical issues. The most important thing is that your child should be healthy and pain-free so he or she can be available to learning. ABA wasn't working on Christian because he was sick. His gut needed to be addressed. His diet needed to be addressed. The toxicity in his body needed to be addressed before he was able to absorb traditional therapies.

Unfortunately, I think a lot of parents are putting faith

in the wrong people. They are listening to the old guard. The whole "woe is me" and "I have to get my son into a home" attitude is still prevalent. That's the problem. There's almost an angry feeling of "I accept it and you should, too." One of the first people at Autism Speaks told me, "It is what it is. There may be improvements and he might learn to potty-train but we have to talk about long-term care and adult homes." I don't want to talk about that! I want to talk about how to help my son be healthy, live in the here and now, and regain his skills. And they looked at me as if I was high on something!

I don't know how long it will be before the CDC hears us and embraces our message. I just got a letter from the director of the Centers for Disease Control, and my husband came home and said, "What are you doing?" I was flailing around the living room, tearing it up.

They keep writing me this dumb letter and it's so stupid. It said, "We are doing everything possible to get to the bottom of this horrible debilitating disease." They are doing nothing except covering their asses. They need to listen to the parents and stop the secrecy because in the end, they're all going to be accountable for this. The tide can't be held back much longer. There is about to be a sea change, and if I were the people at the CDC, I would jump out of the nearest window I could find because I couldn't live knowing what I had done.

WE WERE ABOUT TO GO to print with this book when I got a call from Katie stating that someone from Autism

Speaks who has a child with autism saw me in an interview and a lightbulb clicked on in his head. He felt a very strong urge to help fund research into environmental components such as vaccines and how they may trigger autism. We were both shocked, wondering if this could really be true. They were only words at this point but words are enough to celebrate change and growth in the right direction. In the past, there have been grants submitted and rejected by Autism Speaks, but there is *talk* now and that makes me smile.

I decided then to go to the Autism Speaks Web site, which I never really wanted to visit before because of their history of ignoring biomedical treatment. I was so happy to see them advertise the Green Our Vaccines rally that Jim and I are leading in Washington, DC. Could Autism Speaks finally be coming around? Could they finally be seeing that parents' testimonies are science-based information and need to be researched? Could they finally be listening to the plea of Katie Wright, who has been screaming for help from the organization that her parents started in her own son's name? I want to believe it's all true. Change is in the air. If Autism Speaks is showing improvement, maybe the CDC and the AAP will follow! Let's hold our breath.

20

The Power of Believing

Dear Jenny,

How are we supposed to believe that all of these biomedical treatments even work? I have a large family and to change the diet for everyone is just too hard. Do you really think it's worth trying? I don't want to waste my time, considering I have none to begin with.

Sincerely,
Karen
St. Louis

I'm glad I opened this letter. Karen represents a lot of moms who wonder if it's worth implementing biomedical treatment. I can answer her by saying I have no idea if the diet or biomedical treatments will work on HER children. With so many moms saying there are improvements in their children's health, I figure it's worth looking into. But I want all parents to know that you are not a "bad" parent for not taking on the biomedical treatments. Many kids don't need to. Many can recover through ABA alone. Some moms have even said that they are absolutely fine with the way their children are and that their children don't need to be "fixed." I agree that these kids are beautiful and perfect, but many of them are sick—physically sick—and these are the children I hope to help.

After reading this letter, I began to think about my journey with Evan again. I thought back to when I first found out about biomedical treatments and tried to remember how long it took me to decide to try them. I came up with about two hours of actual wondering, but when I changed my doubts to belief, we were on the road to recovery.

The most powerful tool of a mother who has a child with autism is the power of believing her child will get better. If your mind is constantly second-guessing and questioning the validity of biomedical treatments when so many moms are saying they help, then that is the path you will stay on. You will stay in the unknown. But if you are determined to heal your child and all of your focus is toward that goal, then your path will be with those who have recovered their children. Nowhere else. There is no second-guessing in this direction. There is no trying the diet halfway in this direction. There are NO excuses in this direction. I've seen families with six children incorporate the diet into their lifestyle. There is only focus, determination, faith, and a clear vision of the best possible outcome for the child.

The time is now to help our kids. Now. The treatment

gets better every year, and even though it might not fully re-cover all children, it will at least make them feel better. It tore my insides up when I used to watch Evan injure him-self. I had no idea why he was doing it until I researched the behavior and found it was because he was in physical pain. I focused on fixing that and did.

The movie *The Secret* is a very real thing. It's all about the law of attraction. Picture your child talking; send feel-ings to that picture and think of how wonderful that will be. Picture your child going to a typical school and having typi-cal friends, then send feelings to that picture of how great it will be. Picture your child no longer stimming and feel how great that will be. The law of attraction is indeed a law. Whatever you think and feel is your reality.

So take a look at your thoughts now. Are they negative? Are you second-guessing the possibilities? Or do you have that surge of hope and faith that your child, too, can be healed and get better? That's where you need to stay. That's where you need to keep that dial pointed, in this direction. Because the universe has no other choice than to make that your reality.

21

Samantha Gray: Mother Warrior to Zach

I WAS AT AN AUTISM CONFERENCE meeting moms face-to-face when I noticed this one woman circling me like the gang leader to a group of seagulls. She had a very sweet smile but a look of determination to get to me. She finally found an opening and flew in for her chance. She gave me a big glowing smile and said nonchalantly, "Hi. I recovered my son and also got hit with breast cancer a month after the autism diagnosis." My mouth hung open as I listened to her heartwarming story. Meet Samantha Gray.

THERE ARE TWO BROTHERS and two sisters in my family. Among all of us, we ended up having fourteen girls. Not one boy, until I gave birth to Zach and we finally got ourselves a boy! So, needless to say, from day one he was like the prince of the family.

He was just the greatest baby. Really even tempered.

And I remember saying, "Oh my God, he's going to talk early." He had great eye contact, the whole bit. Then after about eighteen months, things changed. Periodically, he would have screaming fits. That was my first signal that something wasn't right.

Time went on and he began talking. He knew his letters, his alphabet, his shapes, and all sorts of things. So we were thinking he was doing very well. Then he started having more temper tantrums for no reason. It wasn't as if somebody did something to him or he wanted something. He just all of a sudden would go into a huge temper tantrum.

And then periodically he would throw up. I would notice at night that he had thrown up in his bed, and I thought maybe it was the milk. We had him on vitamin D milk at that time. So I thought, "Well, maybe I'll reduce it to 2 percent." Of course, my husband, Gary, didn't want that because he's a doctor, an internist, and said milk was good for Zach, so I continued giving him milk.

Then the throwing up got worse. He'd be sitting in his high chair and would actually projectile-vomit, and once he did, he would be okay. So I knew he wasn't sick with a virus or anything in particular. And the temper tantrums started getting really severe. He would arch his back and then bite really hard. Finally, I knew something was going on, something was wrong. It wasn't Zach.

Next he became very sensitive to sound. So I started researching on the computer about kids who hold their hands over their ears, and all of a sudden "Asperger" came up. Asperger? What's that? So I looked it up and I started reading about it. "He doesn't have that," I thought. In the information about Asperger's I saw the word "autism." I said to myself, "Oh, he doesn't have autism," but I read about it anyway.

I clicked on "autism" and read all the criteria. There were categories so you could see if certain characteristics match. Something like twenty things matched. And I was reading it and screaming, "Oh my God." I thought I was going to pass out. All I could do was panic. "Oh my God! He has autism! Oh my God!" I knew right then, there was no doubt in my mind, Zach had autism.

Of course, the site that I happened to go on first was the site that had the extremely gloomy outcomes. Children with autism are not going to live on their own. They're not going to have kids. They're not going to get married. And I was thinking my son was supposed to be the football star, all these sports, he's our boy. The boy everyone waited for.

I was devastated. I couldn't think straight. A little time later, Gary came in. My husband is the physician who freaks out about everything. You wouldn't think so, being that he's a physician, but he's the freak-out person in the family. I was thinking, "Oh, God, do I tell him? Do I not tell him? Should I go to the doctor first? What do I do?"

For something like this I couldn't wait. I just couldn't because I was so distraught.

He came into the room and looked at me, and I said,

"Oh my God, I have something to tell you." He asked what was wrong, but I could barely speak. I was sobbing. "Zach... has...autism."

Gary looked at me and said, "No, he doesn't."

But I insisted, "Yes, he does. I just read all about it. He's got autism."

My husband was thinking I was totally crazy. He said, "There is no way he has autism," and then he started going off, going crazy.

Finally, I said, "Well, he has his wellness appointment in a few days so I'll check with the pediatrician."

I went to the doctor by myself. I decided I wasn't going to say one word to the doctor because I wanted him to make the diagnosis, not me. I was going to pretend that I didn't know anything. At the appointment, I didn't say anything, and then the doctor asked if I had any concerns. I said, "Well, yes, I do. Zach has been throwing some tantrums, he's vomiting, and he puts his hands over his ears a lot."

The doctor looked at me. "Well, I need to refer you to a neurologist."

So I called and made the appointment with the neurologist. I would bring my babysitter with me because Gary still wouldn't come. He still didn't believe any of this whatsoever.

We got to the neurologist and Zach just sat and rolled his toy car back and forth, basically doing nothing. The doctor talked to Zach for a little bit. Then he told me that Zach has autistic spectrum disorder.

"Yes, I know." I'd already been crying my eyes out. I knew what it was, so the diagnosis didn't surprise me.

He said I could get some training and call for services. He added, "If he gets out of control, there are some drugs we can put him on."

At the very end he told me, "By the way, insurance doesn't cover any of this."

And I said, "What?" He probably thought I was a crazy person, because when he told me my son's diagnosis I didn't say anything. But when he told me insurance didn't cover it, I freaked out. "Well, why not?" I asked him.

He responded, "Because they consider it a preexisting condition and it's not covered by insurance." I just couldn't grasp that.

So I took the little handwritten piece of paper that he gave me, and I went home. When my husband came home I told him, "Yes, he does have autism." Gary was very weird about it. He simply didn't want to talk about it at all. I knew the next person I had to tell was my oldest daughter, who was seventeen. I remember telling her that Zach had autism and we both cried and cried and cried. It was a touching thing. We hugged each other all night, I and my daughter.

The next day I cried and cried some more. And then I thought, "Okay, I've got to look all this stuff up, and I've got to call all these places. I've got to see what I even need to do, because nobody tells you what to do." They tell you your child's going to need all these therapies, but who do you even call?

I had to read about this. I needed to learn. So I immediately went to Borders and bought four books, a couple of them actual ABA books.

As I was reading all about the ABA therapy, I learned that a child will need forty hours of treatment a week. And I thought, "Forty hours times 250 dollars. I can't do that! We don't have that much money. There's no way."

My husband was now reading a little bit here and there but still not really talking about it that much. I tried to talk to him, but he was still in denial and, I guess, completely depressed about the whole thing. He was trying to think of all the medical reasons that Zach had this. So I was not really able to lean on him or get much support from him at this point.

I said I was going to start the ABA program myself, because, of course, I always think I can do everything. There's nothing I can't do! I can do anything! If I have to do these forty hours by myself, I will do it.

The very first thing I did was "drop block." I will never forget it. I got a huge tub that the big LEGOs come in and I would say to Zach, "Drop block," and then I would drop the block. And he did it eventually. I was thinking, "Oh my God, he dropped the block! He dropped the block!" I was so excited. I was thinking how great this is, that I'm going to work through the whole program. At this point I was feeling pretty good.

Then two weeks later, I felt a lump on my breast. It was weird. I'd never had anything like it.

I thought I'd better tell Gary. I acted as if it was no big

deal. I said, "Can you feel this? What do you think? Could it be something?" I could tell he was freaking out in his mind but he wouldn't tell me. So I went for my mammogram and ultrasound and then sat in the waiting room. Finally, the poor doctor who had to be the bearer of bad news came out. "Can I talk to you?" I thought, "Okay, here it comes." She said, "Well, we do think there's cancer there."

I really didn't do anything. I just said, "Okay, what do I need to do?" I was very calm about it. I didn't have that much emotion right then. Not until more tests came back and they told me it was an aggressive type of cancer and that I would have to have a mastectomy, immediately followed by chemotherapy and radiation.

Then I freaked out. That was a Wednesday, and I was in surgery on Friday, getting the thing removed. I kept telling myself, "I just have to get this done because I need to take care of my son. He needs me, and I can't be sick."

I did what I needed to do. In the meantime, my mom, Gary's mom, my sitter, and my family went into extreme helping mode. I would say to them, "No matter what you do, play with him, talk to him. I don't care what you do with him. It doesn't have to be any formal game or whatever. I don't care. You've just got to be doing something at all times."

We were just trying to keep him busy. I ordered every flash card I could find online, from every single company you can imagine. I thought, if there's nothing else I can do than lie in this bed, then I can do flash cards with him, because he loves to do flash cards. That was my mission while going through cancer with chemotherapy. I was the flash card person. That's what I did.

I still didn't know anything about biomedical treatments at this point. Right after Zach was diagnosed, I read something about the gluten-free, casein-free diet. And I thought, "Oh, God, that would be so hard." Zach drinks a gallon of milk a day. There was no way I could take this child off milk. He loves milk. That's all he will drink and my husband really wanted to keep him on milk. I was freaking out about this diet thing but I thought maybe, just maybe I would be willing to try it.

So I told Gary, "You know, they talk about the gluten- and casein-free diet."

And he said, "Well, first of all, I think it's crazy, but there's a test we can do and I'll just tell his doctor to run it." The test was to see if Zach is allergic to casein and gluten. I found out later that it doesn't matter if the child is actually allergic; it has to do with these kids not being able to break down the proteins in dairy and wheat.

But Gary called the doctor and said, "Just humor me and my wife, and please run this gluten casein test, because she's thinking of a gluten- and casein-free diet."

Of course, my pediatrician said, "Oh, that doesn't work. I wouldn't even mess with it."

Gary responded, "Just humor us and run the test."

So he did, and of course my pediatrician and Gary were pleased because the test came back negative for dairy and wheat allergy. So Gary said, "We're not going to do that diet." With the chemo and everything else going on, I just let it go.

I was well into chemo and radiation when Zach started projectile-vomiting really severely. It was becoming more and more frequent, and the tantrums were getting worse. Even though we were doing ABA therapy and saw good things from it, I also saw more deterioration.

His stools—oh my God! This child had the worst stools in the world. Five a day at least, just diarrhea. It was awful. Sometimes seven a day! His poor bottom would be red all the time. I was constantly putting stuff on his bottom to keep it from being red. And with the tantrums, now no one could relate to him anymore.

When I finally finished with chemotherapy and started to feel a little bit better, I was able to take Zach to the pediatrician to get some help for him. I told the pediatrician that he projectile-vomits, that he doesn't have normal stools, he has tantrums all the time, and screams as if he is in pain.

The pediatrician looked at me and said, "Oh, it's just autism."

I asked, "Well, can't you test his stool or test him for anything?"

"No, not really. We don't do that. It's just the way with autistic children."

I was thinking, "No, no! That makes no sense to me."

How could every single thing be going wrong with my son now when he was born perfectly fine? They were telling me this is how he is now, with no medical testing whatsoever? I knew I was going to get to the bottom of this. I wasn't buying it.

Gary was still saying to me, "This is how he's going to be the rest of his life and there's nothing you can do about it." Because again, he was in what I call his "doctor box." He was not coming out of it. So I started reading and reading and reading. I stayed up until three or four in the morning almost every night. All I asked for Christmas that year was an Apple computer. All I wanted to do was my own research because no one else would help me. So I got an Apple laptop. I always say this Apple computer saved Zach's life because I was able to sit up until three, four in the morning in my bedroom without disturbing anyone.

I started typing in everything: "Autism, help and cures, treating autism." And one thing I came across was a story about this kid Miles. He drank milk all the time. He was addicted to milk. Once they took him off milk, the child was unbelievably better. And then it also told about how they started doing some biomedical treatments. And I thought, "This sounds just like Zach."

I took notes. Notes, notes, and more notes. Gary finally said to me, "What are you doing? Why don't you get some sleep? You need to get to sleep."

I said, "I don't care. I am going to find out some things. I keep reading these really interesting things, Gary. I think you need to read them." Gary was still not doing any research on autism. He was still, at that point, pretty much in denial or just settled with what the medical community says, which is that nothing can be done.

Somehow I found Dr. Andrew Wakefield's story and started reading it. Of course there are a lot of things that I don't understand, but, you know, you read between the lines when you're not a physician. You start using common sense. I realized that Zach had gut issues, like leaky gut syndrome.

I printed out Dr. Wakefield's research and I was excited because it had real doctor material in it. It had all the stuff that I knew Gary would understand. I handed it to Gary. "Here. Here is an article. You need to read it."

Well, he read it that night. A normal person reading it would be amazed, as I was, of course. But Gary didn't say a word. Just silence.

But a day and a half later, Gary actually came to me and said, "That article was pretty interesting, I'll have to say." I couldn't believe it! His head had peeked out of the "doctor box" just a little. I was happy that it got him thinking a bit more about the gut connection.

In the meantime, after all my research, I decided to start by ordering some enzymes, colostrum, and vitamins, and to finally start Zach on the gluten-free, casein-free diet. So I told Gary, "I'm taking our son off the milk." He had fought me this whole time, saying that we're not going to take him off milk, that it's good for him and he needs the milk. I said, "I don't care what you say. I'm taking him off of milk today."

That night, I bought every nondairy milk that I could find, rice milk, almond milk, all the stuff that they say is okay to drink. And the next day, I mixed a half-and-half of the milk he was drinking and the new nondairy milk. On the second day, I noticed a difference.

He was going around the house asking me, "What's this? What's that?" Then he came up to me and hugged me. He hugged me! And I felt it inside. It was a real hug! Oh, you can imagine. I was freaking out.

Then I knew I was onto something. This was my sign to keep going. I went onto a Web site that I wound up falling in love with called talkaboutcuringautism.org and I read about an autism conference coming up. I went to Gary and said, "There is a conference in Chicago called Autism One, and I am going to go to this conference."

"Okay, whatever." But then a miracle happened. The next day he started asking me questions about it, and I told him about it, and he said, "All right, we'll go." I wanted to jump up and down and scream. I couldn't believe he said he would go!

Gary and I sat in on every biomedical talk at the conference. I didn't understand most of the stuff they were talking about because there were so many medical terms, but Gary was frantically taking notes. After the third session, he looked at me and said, "Sam, those sons of bitches. I can't believe it. It's fucking true."

"Right, right!"

"Sam, it spoke against everything that I have been taught. I don't even know what to do with this information. I just can't even believe this." He was in total shock. He was livid, so mad that he just kept saying he couldn't believe it.

He was also angry that our pediatrician hadn't told us anything about this.

We came home and Gary was still overwhelmed, but he dove into studying everything in the biomedical world, and I mean everything! We got a DAN! doctor to guide us through and tested Zach for everything. We implemented many things, including chelating, and saw improvement after improvement.

Now Zach just turned five and goes to a mainstream preschool for four-year-olds, exactly the grade he should be in, and goes there every day, five days a week. I have not had one complaint from the teacher.

My husband has a hard time going to work now. He would love to be a DAN! doctor but we're not in a position to do that yet because, well, I just found out two weeks ago my cancer is back. They want me to do radiation again, but no way in hell. Chemo nearly killed me and I'm not going through that again.

I would like to tell parents reading this to research every single thing that you can. Do not take what your doctor says or what your neurologist says 100 percent and not go any further. So many parents say, "Well, okay, that's what the pediatrician said, so that's what's going to happen, and that's how my son is going to be from now on." That is not true. I used to say, "If I do this and he just gets 20 percent better— that's wonderful." And you can't just stop. If it's something that you know is not going to hurt your child—a vitamin, a supplement, a treatment—then go for it.

Twenty years from now, if they say, "B12 was it, that was the deal," and I had not tried that, and I knew it was something that wouldn't have hurt my son, I would be devastated. I would be sick that I hadn't tried everything I could try for my kid. And I think that's what parents really need to think about. Because there are a lot of parents I talk to who say, "You know, we're just going to do this. We don't really believe that."

Why are people so reluctant to get all of these tests done and see for themselves? What if your child is too low in something or too high? You won't know unless you test him. It's time to do something, Mom or Dad. These children are physically sick. It is not just in their minds.

I PRAY THAT by the time this book comes out, Samantha will be cancer-free yet again. Her strength during these two battles in her life makes me realize that most problems we have are too small to ever think twice about. She's an amazing warrior and I pray for all moms out there who are dealing with similar battles.

22

God Help Us

IN APRIL 2008 I was on *Larry King Live*. It was the second time I'd been on the show and I'm grateful that Larry continues to have shows on autism. He does such a wonderful job of continually bringing the controversy about autism to the mainstream media in America.

I was amazed that the CDC denied my invitation to join me on the panel. Where the hell are these people? What are they afraid of? What do they have to hide? Fortunately, two members of the American Academy of Pediatrics (AAP) joined me for what I expected to be a heated debate about vaccines and autism. They had put out a press release the day before the show stating that the AAP was going to work with DAN! I hoped it wasn't bullshit. They were just words on a piece of paper at this point but I was hoping AAP would follow through. If they don't, of course, I will hold up their press release on every talk show until my fingers bleed.

While sitting in Larry's studio waiting to go live, I

looked over at the people from AAP and wondered how they could be so blind. I wondered how they could live day to day oblivious to the screams of all these parents. I wish to God the cameras had been rolling during the commercial breaks because the debate continued off air. Dr. David Tayloe from the AAP was telling me how sometimes the parents at his practice don't bring their children in on time for their wellness visits; they bring the kids in when they are sick, so he has no choice but to play "catch-up" and inject them with all the vaccines they had missed. I flew back in my chair, which wheeled across the stage, and Larry shouted to me to come back. I was shocked to learn that not only was the doctor playing catch-up with vaccines but doing it while these kids were sick. The biggest recipe for disaster! I found out later that the phrase he uses is (get ready for this one) Grab 'em and Stab 'em.

Yes, Grab 'em and Stab 'em. This man, by the way, is the president of the American Academy of Pediatrics! God help us all.

23

Stan Kurtz: Warrior Dad of Ethan

REMEMBER STAN THE MAN? He was the dad who helped me during my press tour. He was the one who made the first call to the AAP on my behalf. Since then, Stan has not stopped working to turn the AAP around. He is also on the Defeat Autism Now! Executive Council and a participant at their think tanks. I highly suggest grabbing a highlighter for Stan's story. I respect everything he has to say and he did an amazing job educating himself and others on how he healed his boy. This is Stan's story.

I HAVE VERY spotty memories of my childhood. My father didn't want a third child. I know I was an accident and if it weren't for my mother, I probably wouldn't be here.

I was really different from my two brothers. I was known in the family as the kid who was bothersome and always trying to figure things out. Looking back now, I'm grateful for it because it helped me heal my son, Ethan.

When I was around ten years old, my mother was diagnosed with cancer. It was devastating. She was the only person who understood me. She was my connection.

Later she had to wear a wig, had a distended belly, and you could see the life was gone from her eyes. It killed me. It really fucked me up.

I was stealing my father's car in the middle of the night just to spend time with her in the hospital room. Most of the time I didn't know if she knew I was there. The pain from the cancer became intense. I remember holding her hand and praying for her pain to go into me.

She died the day I was playing hooky from school. I didn't cry. I didn't even cry at the funeral. It took me years to actually mourn her death, and I still believe I left a huge part of me with her in that hospital room that day. I loved her more than anything, and the fact that I couldn't heal her paralyzed me.

As I grew older, I really yearned for a family of my own. I looked hard and long to find that one special person whom I could start a family with and commit myself to for the rest of my life. Then I met Michelle. We became friends over the phone and the Internet and I thought to myself when I first saw her, "Wow, she's really beautiful." I asked her to marry me six months later. She already had a fourteen-year-old daughter but knew of my yearning to have a child, so she agreed to have just one. I was just so excited and grateful.

The night of our honeymoon, I worked really hard to make the room as romantic as I could, but she completely trumped me with the best gift ever. She handed me her birth control pills. It was the best gift a guy could ever get. Well, if you want to have a kid, anyway. We waited a few months like you're supposed to and then on our first try she got pregnant. Everything was perfect and good.

I was very excited to be a dad. I watched every second of the delivery. I was enthralled. I was kind of in shock until we got into the elevator and I saw him bundled up in that blanket like a burrito. I thought, "Here is my baby boy. He's finally here." My heart almost tore open with the amount of love that was going through it. Then Ethan became jaundiced on the second day, so they put him under the lights and it was a few days until we were able to bring him home.

Coming home was awesome. The only problem we really had was that Michelle and I would fight about who got to change his diaper and hold him. She wanted to do everything her way with him and it was hard for her to relinquish control. I honestly would beg to change his diaper.

Then around six months later, I remember looking at Ethan sitting in his little saucer thing and Michelle was talking to me and said "Wow," and then suddenly Ethan said "Wow," then she said "Wow," and he said "Wow," and it was amazing to watch him say his first word. It was so freakin' awesome!

As the year went on, everything seemed to be perfect in my eyes but not Michelle's. Ethan was eleven months old and she began noticing delays. She was afraid to be the one to tell me what she was seeing. We took him to the next appointment with the pediatrician and he said that everything was fine.

At sixteen months Ethan still wasn't walking, talking, or pointing. When I wasn't around, Michelle called the pediatrician and demanded a referral. The doctor told Michelle, "I don't think there is anything wrong, but I'll give you the referral if you really want."

So we went to one of the best developmental pediatricians for a formal evaluation. She did her stuff, looked at Ethan, and said, "He's on the autism spectrum."

"Sorry?" I was completely stumped by what she had said to us. She must have seen by the look on my face that I was in denial. She then went on to perform a hard-core reality check on me.

She said, "Did you notice that he hardly came over to you both during this session? That's not typical. Did you see how he couldn't play with that car in a way that was appropriate? It's not normal for his age." She went through thing after thing after thing, and after each individual example we couldn't deny it, because she was right. I knew Ethan had these little eccentricities but I just didn't know what it all added up to. So she took the equation apart and did the math for me. She said, "See how long he's been staring out that window?" And I could feel my heart sinking as I looked over and saw my son staring out the window, expressionless.

I uttered, "He stares out the window all the time."

She said, "That is not typical."

I REMEMBER WHEN Evan used to do that. I called him Buddha when he used to stare out the window because it was as if he was in deep meditation. He wouldn't respond to any noises and just stared and stared. I remember thinking, "Wow, my kid is deep. He really is in his own meditation."

I WAS FLASHING BACK and flashing forward. I was watching my mind play back each thing happening ten times here, ten times there, and it was *boom*! Here we are, holy shit, autism. I became two inches smaller in my chair. I thought for sure all the blood was sucked out of my body and I was just sitting there as a skeleton with nothing left, paralyzed. My image of our future was a life of pain, challenges, work, and incredible suffering. I felt my dreams for Ethan slipping away. I was left feeling I have defective sperm.

Yeah, I felt as if I lost my kid. He was gone. Everything that was in my head about him was dead. It is terrible to say, but I felt I was with a completely different child then. After hearing the diagnosis, it was as if there was a starship that beamed Ethan out of the room and replaced him with a child who has autism. And now I'm looking at a kid I've never seen before.

Once we went home, I climbed into my bed. It felt as if I stayed there for a month. I sank into a depression. Michelle was running Ethan from therapy to therapy. Stuff just happened around me. When I did get up, I dragged myself around like a zombie.

At this point, Ethan was twenty months old. He had very fleeting eye contact and he had no speech. He would just play with the same toy or watch the wheels on his truck go around and around.

I felt so worthless not being able to engage my son. I felt I was put in the middle of a forest with no path. There was no light. There was no instant gratification. That's a big deal for guys. We love instant gratification, and there was so little. Usually, you do something and you get a result from your child. I wasn't getting much at all, and at the time I thought that's the way it would always be.

At this point, it was hard even to look at him. It's not that I didn't want to look at him. I didn't look at him and think, "Yuck, he's a deformed kid." It was just that my love to look at him wasn't there. I felt terrible. I was just so sorry that I couldn't help him, and then I felt guilty of course, because I'm the one who wanted to have a kid. So I'm like, fuck! We're here because I made Michelle do this. It's my fault. This happened right in front of me, on my watch and I couldn't protect him. For as long as I could remember, I had wanted a child, and I turned out to be the worst father on the planet.

Finally someone mentioned something to me about Defeat Autism Now! and other conferences and suggested that I might want to go. I had no idea about them so I decided to check one out. This was about four months after we got Ethan's diagnosis.

I was just getting out of my own depression, realizing, "Okay, I'm going to survive this and things are okay." And I started to understand that Ethan was still the same kid. He wasn't beamed away; it was just my imagination. Actually, I was the one who was beamed away.

So I started to go to autism conferences. I think guys need to go to conferences because then they have something to do to get their hands around it all. After going to them, you start to realize that there are biological reasons for the things that earlier you had decided just to accept as part of your child. You first struggle through your denial to see simply the shell of autism, but when you go to the conference, you start learning what is on the inside that causes the shell to act the way it does.

It changed everything for me. I was learning, "Oh, I can try this and I can try that and look for a result." I was hearing, "Here are the areas where we commonly see issues with autism, and here is something you can actually do for your individual child's needs." I was thinking, "There are things you can actually do?" I looked around the room, trying to figure out how other people were taking all this in, wondering if I was the only one here totally fucking shocked—that is, angered that no one had told us.

I wasn't one of those people who said, "Oh, this has got to be bullshit." My instincts were screaming that this was right. I was looking at it like the science that it so obviously was. I was starting to learn about certain toxins and what harm they can do, such as the ones in vaccines. How the metabolism and immune system responds and how it can cause the autism effect. I was just sitting there thinking, "That makes a lot of sense." There are other conditions where metabolic, toxic, and infectious issues cause problems in the body and the brain. As soon as I started learning about that, I had no problem believing how it was all connected. So I just kept with it and then I became addicted to learning more and more.

I remember thinking, "If this is the case, if learning teaches me more about my child and that can lead to him getting better, there is nothing else that I want to do." All the other stuff in my life was meaningless, trivial. I couldn't think of anything else. I didn't want to do anything else. I didn't want to work. So I stopped everything, and learning became my full-time job. My new job was to save my son. I was absolutely 100 percent mono-focused and said good-bye to my friends and anybody else who didn't want to talk only about autism and the recovery of Ethan. When people talked to me about remodeling their kitchen or something like that, I remember thinking, "Who the hell cares about your kitchen!"

So I studied and studied. I even posed as a doctor to crash a physicians' training. A year went by and I still hadn't implemented anything yet because I was scared shitless. I didn't want to make a mistake and fuck things up worse.

My wife, Michelle, this whole time was watching me obsessively learn, but she was not into biomedical at all. She was too overwhelmed to change anything else. After a year of educating myself had gone by, I remember being downstairs in front of the computer finishing some reading that supported how safe the diets are and I said to myself, "I'm ready now, we're starting tomorrow, here we go!" So I started running up the stairs like Rocky Balboa and I burst into the kitchen and said, "Honey, guess what, we're going to start the diet tomorrow!"

She just looked at me and without hesitation said, "No! We're not."

I stopped in my tracks, not believing what she had said. Then she started cleaning the house. She couldn't bring herself to look at me and she was giving me a "get the fuck away from me" energy like you can't imagine. You know, an energy that said "there's no way you're getting near my child." It was the same kind of energy when she wouldn't let me change Ethan's diaper.

I was completely shocked, actually. It's hard enough when your family and friends don't believe, but not even your wife? It was the last thing I expected. It was as if she'd punched me in the groin. I didn't know how to respond. There was no back-and-forth about it.

When we did begin arguing about the diet, we went on for weeks. I was beside myself.

When you can't convince your spouse, it's the worst feeling ever. At my wits' end, I finally went to Michelle and said, "Honey, I'm going to divorce you and then I'll be able to do biomedical interventions on Ethan half the time and he'll have the diet at least half the time. This is not what I want, but I can't live like this. I need to be able to look him in the face when he's twenty-one and tell him I did everything I could."

Later that day she walked over and said, "Okay, let's do it. We'll just do it. Let's just do it."

At first I thought, "Oh, thank God," but then thought, "Oh, God, please let this work!"

I DECIDED TO E-MAIL Stan's wife, Michelle, and ask her why she had been hesitant about the diet. It's common that one parent is not completely on board and I wanted to hear her point of view. She told me that it was so foreign to her. She grew up on wheat and milk and never considered it to be a bad thing. She said that the diet seemed as if she would be doing a disservice to Ethan because those were the things you give a child to be strong and healthy.

This is such a common belief with people when, in actuality, *not* being on the diet can cause major harm to these kids.

So WE DID SOME shopping and Michelle totally got on board. After a couple of days I thought I started seeing something. It wasn't huge; it was just something. Ethan looked clearer and I was seeing a little more eye contact.

Then in two weeks he was literally doubling his language. Michelle also took notice, and at that point, I think her beliefs began to change. I think that's when we stopped battling each other and started becoming partners in the battle together.

Every little thing Ethan did was an exciting accomplishment. Yet there were always constant reminders that even though he was making progress, we still had a long way to go. For example, we have a bird named Harry. Ethan would point to Harry and say "bird" and we'd be so excited!

Then our next-door neighbor Sophie, who was born at the same time as Ethan, came over and said, "Oh, look at Harry. I like his little yellow beak and how his feet kind of go 'click click click' back and forth, and he takes his food and he puts it in the water and he puts it back in the food and then he eats it." And all I could think was, "Please stop talking, Sophie, please. Just put a knife through my heart." Hearing her speak so well made me depressed again. She reminded us how far behind we still were.

So then we got Ethan started on some supplements and arranged to get an Organic Acid Test (OAT) and Comprehensive Food Allergy Profile and other testing that the traditional pediatricians know hardly anything about. The results came back with abnormal levels of candida, a nasty fungus. Ethan also had twenty-one food hypersensitivities, low Krebs cycle and energy functioning, possible mitochondrial problems, eight metabolic abnormalities, high levels of uranium in his hair, low excretion of mercury, high levels of copper, and low levels of zinc.

Physically he had sensory issues, low awareness of pain, low muscle tone, severe ankle pronation, dark puffy eyes, red cheeks, distended belly, pale and dry skin, pronounced right-side muscle weakness, sensitivity to light, little eye contact, obsessive and perseverative behaviors, and what appeared to be mini-seizures.

We were gluten- and casein-free. We had a trajectory of

some gains and then he flattened out. I was building my confidence in what I could see and in trusting my instincts, but what I now saw was a total flat line in Ethan's development. We were maybe two months into the diet and I knew something wasn't right. I said to Michelle, "We have to re-test him and see what's going on." So we redid the OAT and found he had less candida but now he had high markers for clostridia—a nasty bacteria linked to autism-like symptoms in animal studies.

I thought to myself, "We are doing the diet, which is supposed to help him. How can another infection in the gut happen like that? How are we seeing a marker for high bacteria when before it was fine? It happened for a reason. What's the reason? How did it happen? I don't get it." So I called the lab and said, "Okay, give me the executive director. Give me the guy in charge." I wanted to know what causes this. His response: complex sugars. Things like rice and pasta. And then he trailed off and I was half listening to him.

I said, "Rice? Like rice milk?"

"Oh, yeah, rice is bad because it feeds bacteria like this."

So, complex carbs are feeding this? Great. Most of the GFCF diet is rice, so now we have to take that away?

That's when I started learning about the Specific Carbohydrate Diet (SCD), which involves removing foods that are disaccharides or polysaccharides, that is, foods made up of complex sugars. These include starches like potatoes and complex carbohydrates like rice and pastas. Corn is a poly-saccharide, a complex sugar; table sugar is a disaccharide, very hard to digest and much easier for bad bacteria and fungus to eat. So basically you are talking about a meat and vegetable diet and some nuts and fruit, too. I also decided to take out his major IgG (immunoglobulin G) food allergies, which were bananas, eggs, and a few other foods.

At this point, luckily, he was doing well enough that Michelle said, "Okay, it's extra work but we'll give it a shot." And as soon as we made these changes, his positive trajectory returned. He started climbing and climbing. All of his autism symptoms lessened; more speech, more spontaneous language, and more eye contact. Every few days, we could see more and more accomplishments. It was great. He was clearly still autistic, but he had gains that we could see and that everybody told us about as well.

We also started using a lot of probiotics (dietary supplements containing good bacteria), including those known to help clostridia, such as Culturelle. Ethan's menu of supplements at this point went like this: Lots of vitamin C, zinc, cod liver oil, L-carnitine, CoQ10, B5, DMG, Super Nu-Thera, an amino acid complex, probiotics, and Epsom salts baths every night. We also tried homeopathic thuja and belladonna. We added each thing one at a time to make sure there wasn't a negative reaction. We tried methyl B12 shots on him because so many children were doing so well on it. But not so, Ethan. Methyl B12 nasal spray worked fabulously on my ADHD symptoms and irritable bowel, but for Ethan it didn't seem to work at all at this point. When we wanted to know for sure if something was really working, we took it away and put it back several times and watched the behaviors change. This is a relatively undeniable scientific way to show these interventions work.

I knew to keep moving forward and every time I went to another conference, I would grab a doctor or a researcher and rattle off what I knew and what I researched and then ask what I was missing. I wanted them to tell me something that I was missing that had recovered a child, because that was all I cared about.

Dr. Bill Shaw is the executive director of Great Plains Laboratory and was working in a vendor booth at a Defeat Autism Now! conference when I walked up to him and asked him those same questions. He said, "Viruses. You need to check out viruses."

"Viruses?"

"Yeah, there are people who go after viruses."

I didn't know where or how viruses came into play. I just thought, "All right, I'll check that out." So I began research on the viral stuff and I was like, "Oh my god! A viral pattern!" An ongoing infection can mimic a lot of the biochemistry that we see in autism.

Then I started looking at the medical literature and found there are cases of late-onset autism at age fourteen and age thirty-one from a herpes virus. A fourteen-year-old girl gets a virus and *bang*: She's autistic. A thirty-one-year-old man, *boom*: autistic.

As early as 1981 there was medical literature talking about medical treatments and the reversal of autism. How the fuck doesn't everybody know this? All you have to do is go into PubMed, a free search engine for accessing MED-LINE, the database of peer-reviewed medical literature sponsored by the National Institutes of Health. When you type in "autism and viruses" or "autism and herpes," you will find these cases immediately. So I was thinking, "I can't believe this! This is insane!"

Viruses and other infections can trigger autism and so can toxins like the ones from vaccines. And in my son, I believe it was both. We were really scared to start Valtrex, which is traditionally an antiviral for herpes viruses, but we did. Ethan had never tested positive for a virus, but I felt it was important to try it. I was scared because I had heard reports that some kids with autism had huge regression, but it was often what I began calling a healing regression, an initial regression during the healing process. We also started Ethan on Diflucan, then Nizoral, medications to treat his candida (a type of fungus), which can flare up during antiviral therapy. I was really afraid. But I had a game face in front of my wife at all times: "It's fine, honey. It's going to be fine."

So we started him on quarter doses and immediately saw a regression. It was a scary regression, scary. Worse than I would have thought.

He became a poop smearer. That was the pinnacle of it. He would smear poop on the wall. He had never done that before. The thing I noticed is that you know most of your child's autistic traits and let's say he has about twenty of them. Well, during this regression time, if you put them on a chart, you would see that they all move up at the same time. That is what this healing regression does—all the negative things look worse. It's as if you have taken the autism volume and turned it up.

This part of the biomedical treatment felt different to me. It felt as if we were mobilizing something and that it was clearing out of his body. I think this change is a response to a new cycle of health and detoxification at the same time: a change in his body's metabolism and immune system and then *poof*! Toxins are finally released from the body. This is how I saw it.

So his eye contact became worse, his speech regressed, his behavior regressed; he became more irritable. I kept saying to my wife, "It is going to be fine. It is all part of the process," and then I would go to the other room and I would pray and cry, "Please don't hang me out to dry here. I'll help as many kids as I can. I will do whatever it takes!"

Then I started to notice little developments in the middle of the regression. Ethan was playing with toys slightly differently. He was looking around differently. There were new cognitive gains.

Then a rash broke out on his face and moved down his body. It was kind of a hopeful sign, because it wasn't a full-body rash that would indicate he's allergic to the medicine. It was just a regionalized rash that didn't itch, and every day it seemed to move down a little bit. And it changed colors during the day. It was darker and lighter throughout the day. Finishing week two, the rash was around his belly and the diarrhea started. Just diarrhea, diarrhea, diarrhea, diarrhea. And then it finally stopped at day twenty or twenty-one. And right in the middle of day twenty-one he looked...energetically he looked different. And I thought, "Wow. Let me grab my camera." So I started filming him, and our housekeeper happened to be over my shoulder watching.

Then Ethan pointed to his doggy music box on the wall and said, "What's this?"

Now, I know he knows what it is. So in that moment, I was thinking, "That's really peculiar. He's never asked me about anything before!" He had about nine hundred hours of therapies at this point, so he sometimes might label something by saying "dog," but now for the first time he asked, "Daddy, what's this?"

I said, "That's a doggy."

And he said, "A doggy. Right," as if he was saying, "You've got it, Dad. Great job." He had never done this before. I was sitting there dumbfounded, my mouth open, just trying to hold myself together, and then he said, "Do you like music?"

I said, "Yeah. I like music."

He asked, "Do you want to dance?"

In my mind I was thinking, "Are you kidding me?" I said, "Yeah!" I was so happy that our housekeeper was there. I handed the camera over for her to video and we looked at each other, making eye contact as if to say, "What the hell's going on?"

And so Ethan and I...we danced. Both of us in our pj's, we danced. I wanted to dance with him forever. I did not want the night to end. I thought it was absolutely amazing. We danced, and we played. I remember holding him tight while he was going to sleep and thinking, "Oh my God! Don't go away. Please don't leave me."

I remember looking at him, thinking everything about him was different. The autism looked gone, as if he'd just finished pooping it out of him. He was still delayed but, to me, seemed normal. And then it got better and better.

I believe these kids want to correct themselves, and they are looking for us to help them along. Some traditional doctors argue that kids sometimes spontaneously get better and that's what actually happens while parents are trying various treatments. Can something like this just go away? As a child grows up, her body grows larger compared to the toxic load. Can that help? Of course it can. Can a kid have an infection that doctors can get somewhat under control? Yes. Can a thousand things happen? Sure. But the amount of evidence that we have of how often we've gotten kids better through improving their health is much greater than what can happen by chance. In fact, without treatment, most children continue to suffer, and a lot of these kids get worse. And how about the diet? How come in only two weeks Ethan doubled his speech? How can he look completely recovered in twenty-one days of doing antiviral and antifungal therapy? I just can't buy that it was a coincidence, two and three times in a row.

Autism is a combination of infections and toxins that can ultimately lead to a neurological breakdown. It could be many types of infections: bacterial, fungal, viral. In the medical literature, I found thirty-one peer-reviewed articles discussing infections in autism. One example is a recent

California study that found children with autism are sixteen times more likely to have mycoplasma, chlamydia, or herpes virus 6. And that's just three of the many infections these kids can have. There are also studies showing that viral infections cause toxic metals to move to the brain. Other studies show that certain commonly undiagnosed bacterial infections in these children's guts can make toxins like mercury even more toxic.

As for toxins, there is substantial scientific evidence that they can get into our kids from vaccines, pesticides, foods, flame retardant materials, and other environmental exposures, and some of it can also come in utero, during pregnancy. It sounds like I'm rattling off a lot of things, but the reality is that there are a lot of ways to get to autism. We just think of autism as one bucket, and it sort of is, in a way. But there are many ways to get you there. Cancer is not so different that way.

In Ethan's case, my son was born with eczema, which I now know is an infection that often starts in the gut. Maybe that infection came from my passing my gut issues to my wife back then. Yes, sperm can carry bacteria and fungus, too. Sexy, right? Added to that, we were feeding Ethan difficult-to-digest foods that feed infections, such as cow's milk, wheat, and complex carbohydrates. His immune system was already kind of jeopardized from the infections, and his ability to detox was compromised. So when the toxins came in, it was as if the immune system said, "I'm over here working on these infections, so whatever toxins from vaccines and the environment come in right now, good luck! because I'm busy over here with these infections."

Ethan's development was delayed and then after his vaccines, he seemed to take a greater downslide. So I think the increase in his toxic load combined with his existing infections is what brought him to autism. For some kids, maybe it's toxins alone that get them there. For others, like Ethan, maybe it's infections and toxins combined.

People tell me the biomedical treatments don't work. I usually hear that from a doctor who has not been to a Defeat Autism Now! conference and is not treating children with autism, or from a parent who may have tried something that didn't work on their child. Sometimes their motto is, "If it doesn't work on my kid, it can't work on any, and I need to attack you if it works on yours." I don't know why that is. It's a weird human nature thing, like they don't want to be left alone in autism.

But I think a majority of cases of autism can be prevented. Take the toxins out of vaccinations and lessen the number of vaccines. Limit the child's exposure to toxins in the environment, such as pesticides and heavy metals. Studies have linked both to causing autism. Why that's not front page news, I have no idea. Check moms and dads for the common infections that we find in these kids before they have children. Get the family on organic diets and get the milk, wheat, and many complex carbohydrates out of the house. Stop using chemical-based pesticides. Have dental amalgams (50 percent mercury) safely removed using rubber dental dams and nasal oxygen. Moms might consider taking the vitamins and supplements that we often give these children, like vitamins C, D, and K, zinc, cod liver oil, and magnesium.

And it might be a good idea for moms to stay away from flu shots containing mercury and at least lessen vaccines to the kids until they are made safe and/or toxin-free. Parents know that it's time they make vaccines safe for all children, not just the lucky ones who happen to be healthy and good at detoxing.

My biggest pet peeve is when people say that genetics are involved in every condition in one way or another. It's partly true, but I think it's a cop-out. I would like the focus to be on the overall health status of the child when he or she encounters toxins in vaccines and in the environment. That is by far the greatest susceptibility and the biggest secret about autism.

Today, Ethan is in a mainstream school and is in first grade with no shadow. He continues some occupational therapy for some fine motor development. We will continue to do diet and some vitamins. We also do hyperbaric oxygen a few times a month and we may someday consider some chelation, depending on his mitochondria tests and how his muscle tone continues to develop. He is doing fabulously and we are proud of him and so grateful.

ETHAN WAS OFFICIALLY undiagnosed by age six, and I hope one day Ethan will know how his dad never stopped believing and fighting to get him back, against all odds.

FOR MORE INFORMATION about Ethan's recovery and
Stan Kurtz's work, visit www.recoveryvideos.com.

Photo by Lisa Markinson

24

Committing

I ASKED MY SISTER JOJO to read Stan's piece after I was done writing it. I wanted her to read it because for the past ten years, she has been suffering from the same candida and parasite issues as kids with autism. We both say that if she was vaccinated with the thirty-six required vaccines now, she would definitely become autistic. She has been on and off of the GFCF diet and antifungal medications for years. When she read Stan's piece, she started crying and said that it completely shifted her perspective. It made her come to a realization.

I couldn't understand, why now? Why after reading Stan's piece? Why not after watching me fight for Evan? She said she realized the difference between how she was trying to heal herself and how these warrior parents healed their kids.

Imagine a warehouse that has a hundred different floors and inside the warehouse there are no lights. It's pitch-black and you can't see a thing in front of you. Everyone has to work their way down each floor in order to get to the exit. The warrior parents step into this warehouse and shut the door behind them. They make the decision to fully commit to going into the unknown and finding their way down each floor until they reach the exit—the exit being recovery or making their kid better.

My sister said she entered the warehouse but wouldn't close the door behind her. She kept leaving it propped open. She couldn't commit. She would start the diet but cheat. She would start certain detox programs and then quit. She blamed doctors for things not working, when all it would have taken was for her to fully commit and close the door behind her. She needed to not be scared of the darkness inside the warehouse and of not knowing which direction to go. She needed to follow her intuition. To keep the faith, like these parents do.

After reading Stan's story, she closed the door behind her and has fully committed to healing herself. No more excuses, no more using food as a reward for her pain or a hard day. She said there is no turning back and plans someday to tell her story of how she made it through that warehouse. She hopes that many parents will join her after reading this.

25

Branson's Miracle

Dear Jenny,

My son, Branson, was perfectly fine until I took him to the doctors. They gave him his shots on the day after his first birthday. At fifteen months, the slide into hell began. He lost his speech, his ability to point or imitate. He lost his sense of balance, his eye contact, and all of his pain receptors. He lost most of his muscle tone and then, tragically, he lost himself. He had diarrhea for six months straight and would scratch himself all over until he bled. His behavior became wild and he no longer would turn in response to his own name. The diagnosis for my only child: regressive autism.

I lay in the laundry room and buried myself in a heap of dirty clothes and literally howled until I thought my soul would break. There really are no words to describe the first time you admit in your heart that your child is gone. Only another parent who has watched their beloved child go from a normal and happy one-year-old to an empty shell could possibly understand this.

How do you mourn a child who is still alive?

You don't. You put on your battle gear and go to war! Every morning I would lie in bed and envision myself standing in the middle of a misty moor in the hills of Scotland, like Mel Gibson in the movie *Braveheart*. He looks so invincible when he does that battle cry. I became him with a huge and mighty sword lifted above my head. I would scream up to the heavens…YOU WILL NOT TAKE MY SON! And charge into the mist to slay the invisible dragon called autism. I have never had a doubt in the seat of my soul as to the outcome of this journey. But I had no idea what a formidable opponent autism would be. Branson started the gluten-free, casein-free diet that day. The turnaround was stunning.

Besides all the developmental issues that come with autism, you get slammed with a host of other, more tragic, medical issues. My son has gastrointestinal disease, leaky gut (where the yeast has eaten holes through the entire length of his intestines), massive heavy-metals poisoning, systemic yeast, fungus, eczema, high oxalates, severe food allergies, and a virus and bacterial problem that seems to have stumped even the finest doctors. But we battle on. Branson takes between forty and eighty supplements and medicines a day (still). From the time he wakes up at six A.M. and goes to bed at seven P.M., he takes something every two hours. He has special exercises (like cross training for stroke victims) and baths with four cups of Epsom salts every night for twenty minutes. We use DAN! protocol with the assistance of Applied Kinesiology. We have his head reset with CranialSacral Therapy weekly; we use cold laser treatments; and his strict diet would blow most people away. He does not eat any wheat, milk, sugar, soy, eggs, yeast, and most fruits, and his diet is fully rotated.

We have endured the pain of his detoxing so severely that one morning he could no longer walk. His legs didn't work anymore. That lasted two days; it was the longest two days of my life.

We are forced to save our own children. I spent every day praying that I would not make Branson worse. I knew from the start that if he was to fully recover, I alone would have to do it for him.

At about the year mark, it looked as though my son would be "nonverbal." More than half the children who lose their voices to autism never speak again. But the miracle was to be ours. Within weeks, Branson had hundreds of words...he was talking. The light came back into his eyes and his soul woke up. We had done it. Back to the regional center we went and he was retested and we were told that he was no longer on the autism spectrum. Without a doubt—the best day of my life!

We still are faced with the entire medical after-effects of this disease, but I know in time we will prevail. Some parents who get functional recovery for their kids are never able to fully heal their bodies. We are now in phase II of Branson's integrative recovery program. I have sold my home and now rent so I won't have to go back into the workforce. This is my job. I am his mom.

The average family spends between $30,000 and $70,000 PER YEAR on biomedical treatment for a child in recovery. This is out-of-pocket since insurance does not cover autism.

We have been on the autism roller coaster for almost two years now, and this has been the hardest time of my life. Although I am a single parent, I am not alone. I have had a chance to be reacquainted with God. Not the God you meet in your Sunday best in church, but the God you meet on your kitchen floor at three in the morning.

There is no Ronald McDonald House for us, no wing at Saint Jude's to offer help, or even hope. The parents of a child with autism are left to go the road alone. I am my son's full-time researcher, biochemist, pharmacist, educator, doctor, nutritionist, and chef. I control all aspects of his environment down to the smallest detail. They say that the children who fully recover have fanatical parents. I smiled when I first read this and told my son: "You are so in!" I am fanatical.

We are Coral and Branson Bergmann, the new face of autism in this country.

> With much love and respect,
> Coral and Branson Bergmann
> Warrior Mom and Hero Son

26

Barbara Walters Is Not So Scary After All!

I WAS WATCHING LARRY KING the night his guest was Barbara Walters. Her new book had just come out and I was interested to hear what she had to say. I wondered how she'd conduct herself having to talk about personal issues in her life.

She began talking about her sister, who is mentally retarded. She talked about how difficult it was growing up, when she was often left out of activities because of her sister's condition. She said she had a lot of resentment toward her sister as a result. And then she said something that I swear to God made me fall off of my sofa. She said that she suspected her sister had autism.

I sat there in awe, thinking, "Of course, of course, now I know the reason Barbara was SO angry at me backstage. The shrill, pointed anger toward me was really just personal pain that she had endured her whole life. I was on her show talking about children recovering from autism and couldn't understand for the life of me why it seemed like she wanted to punch me in the face. I get it now. I'm not even upset about it anymore. How can I be?

I can't begin to comprehend what it must be like to be the sibling of a child with autism. I'm sure there will be books written by siblings when this generation of autism grows up, and I'm sure many of them will have the same stories of resentment that Barbara remembers from her childhood. Let's nourish these siblings and listen to them. They may just be the Barbara Walters of the future.

27

Gina Tembenis:
Mother Warrior to Elias

STAN KURTZ CALLED ME in tears one day to tell me about a family he knew of who had gone through hell. When he told me their story, I couldn't believe it. I was with Jim at the time and I had to run away while Stan retold me their heart-wrenching story. I didn't want Jim to see me fall apart, yet again. I closed the door to my bathroom and crunched my body into the corner of the room while I pressed the phone even closer to my ear. I finally told Stan that I couldn't take it anymore. I knew I had to set up an interview with this family. There is a reason Gina is the final warrior in this book. You are about to understand why.

MY HUSBAND, HARRY, and I brought in our son Elias for his four-month wellness appointment. It was December 26, the day after Christmas. My husband was holding him when he got the shots. When the nurse stuck him with the needle, my son just stiffened up like a board and screamed. My husband asked, "What did you give him?" and they ran down the list, four shots for nine different diseases. My husband said, halfheartedly joking, "You know what? That would kill an elephant, let alone an infant." Boy, did he hit the nail on the head, because when we brought him home, the beginning of the worst had begun.

They gave us the precautionary "he might run a fever...a little swelling," the usual "blah blah blah" spiel they give.

So the fact that he was fussy when we put him to bed didn't seem so out of the ordinary. He kept waking up. So I kept going in and checking on him, but he was fine. Harry had to go to work in the morning and asked me if we could turn the monitor off. I said, "No, no, no, don't turn it off. Let's just turn it down low so at least I can still hear him." So Elias finally fell asleep. But then I heard him make this weird noise, so I got up and started walking toward his room. When I walked in, I saw my boy convulsing in his crib. He was having a full-blown seizure.

I started screaming to my husband and he jumped out of bed and we put a blanket around Elias and ran out of the house. There was an ice storm happening but we lived very close to a hospital so we didn't even think to call an ambulance. We just grabbed him and jumped into the car. But when we got into the car, it was frozen. This whole time, Elias was still seizing in my arms. I started to panic and both of us ran to our other car and were desperately trying to get into it.

We finally got in, and now foam was coming out of our

son's mouth. I just kept saying to him, "Stay with me, stay with me, stay with me."

When we pulled up to the hospital, there was a police officer standing outside. We opened the car door and started screaming, "Our baby's seizing!" The police officer took him, and we ran in.

I shouted to them, "I think he's having a reaction to the shots, to the vaccines. He got them today." So they brought me over to the nurse and she asked me what the situation was and I said again, "I think he's having a reaction to the vaccines. He got them today."

He had now been seizing forty minutes.

My husband and I were crazed, pleading, "Oh my god, can't you get him to stop?" There was a wall of people around him working on him. Harry and I were so scared. They kept saying, "His heart's doing okay, though, he's fine. His heart's doing okay." And we kept pleading, "Make the seizures stop!"

They finally got it to stop, but then Elias had partial paralysis. Half of his face looked like he'd had a stroke; one eye, his mouth, and the whole muscle structure of his face were drooped. The other half of his face was fine. I thought at this point he was dead, I hate to say. Because everyone just kind of stepped back, walking away, and I was thinking, "This is not good," especially when I saw his face in that condition. Then one nurse went over and moved his thumb, and it's almost as if it pulled the life back into Elias, because all of a sudden his face corrected itself from the paralysis.

I had never been so scared, never in my life.

We were in the ICU for two or three days and when we finally left, what I had stated to the police officer, to the people registering, to the emergency room staff about the vaccine injury never showed up in any paperwork.

Nowhere was it noted that it was a vaccine reaction. When we went back to our pediatrician and told him that we believed it was because of the shots Elias received that same day, he told us there was in no way any correlation between the seizures and his vaccines. He went on and on and told us not to worry and he did such a good job convincing us that we actually believed him.

Then it happened again. We vaccinated and Elias immediately seized. He seized forty-five times within his first year. It was during this time my husband started researching with Google.

We hadn't gotten to the autism point yet but Harry was coming across things such as B vitamin deficiencies and diet and we wanted to present this to our pediatrician because all that was happening so far was more seizures and all they were doing was either adding drugs or bumping up the dosages of drugs Elias was already taking.

By now Elias was reaching certain milestones. He could sit up when he was supposed to, he could walk when he was supposed to, but at the same time he couldn't point, couldn't wave, and was nonverbal.

He looked right through us as if we were ghosts. He wouldn't respond when his name was called, so we started questioning, Could this be autism? With the research we had begun on Google, the signs started pointing in that direction.

We kept saying to each other, please don't let it be the "A" word. That's what we called it. The "A" word. We were very scared of it because everything we read made it seem as if it was all over. If it was autism, then it was over and done. So we called the children's hospital in Boston because it's one of the leading hospitals. They picked a neurologist for us and we went out there. She examined Elias, and I watched him fail tests and I kept doing what moms do, which is to defend our children. "Oh, he's just having a bad day today. Maybe that's what it is…because you know, he'll say moo, square, rectangle. He knows all his colors."

The neurologist candy-coated her results until my husband asked her to just spill it.

"PDD-NOS," she said.

We were confused for a second and then Harry asked, "Is PDD autism?"

She said, "Yes, it is. Here's a folder with information that you might want to read."

We went back to the car and I took the folder and said, "I'm not looking at that. She's nuts. No way." I went straight into denial.

A month later Elias had five more seizures, one of which required an ambulance because he kept having seizure after seizure. So we decided to concentrate on getting the seizures to stop rather than deal with the whole "A" word right away.

Elias ended up with a lot of seizure medications. He was

taking four at one time, and could barely walk. He stopped seizing but he was a train wreck. He even got to the point where he couldn't move.

I felt totally helpless. The whole thing was just so stressful all the time. If he got sick, I would panic, because if he got a fever, he would end up having a seizure. Fevers can induce seizures.

Elias now moved past PDD-NOS into the full autism diagnosis.

We started to question everything because nothing they were doing was working. There was only so much we could take, watching our son suffer so much.

We started to take matters into our own hands.

January 2004 was when we found our DAN! doctor. He said to start the diet. The gluten-free, casein-free diet. Then he ran the battery of tests that we always wanted but were told no by our pediatrician. The heavy-metals test, the food allergies, yeast, nutritional, everything, the whole nine yards.

It turned out Elias had yeast, his zinc level was extremely low, and he was deficient in B vitamins and minerals such as magnesium, manganese, and chromium. So we started Super Nu-Thera and cod liver oil, eventually an antifungal to kill yeast, methyl B12 shots, and glutathione.

The first improvement we saw was sleep. I went through hell for almost four years with his being up every night. Then his focus got better and the best part of it all was that his seizure count went down. He went from forty-five seizures a year to maybe one or two now.

Then we started him on an antiviral, Valtrex, and speech started pouring out of him. We were blown away. Even his teacher at school asked us what we did to him, because he was totally different. He still had processing problems, but the improvement with speech was amazing. He was also becoming a real ham. It was this great comedic charm that he had, a sense of humor. Things were looking up.

Five months later, a mother's worst nightmare unfolded.

Elias woke up on Thursday morning and had a sore throat and his voice was hoarse, but he didn't have a fever. Later in the day, though, he started to get a fever. And of course I went into panic mode and jumped on the Motrin. Now his breathing began to sound funny. So the next day, I called Harry at work to tell him to come home because I wanted to take Elias to the hospital just to make sure he wasn't getting an infection or something.

I took Elias to the hospital and checked him in. We went into the waiting room, and Elias had a blast, banging on the tables, running around, watching cartoons, playing with stuff. Harry showed up just as we were going into the examining room. They wanted to swab his throat to do a culture, so Harry had to hold him to restrain him a bit. After they swabbed him, the nurse walked out of the room and Elias started having a seizure in Harry's arms.

So I flew out of the room to tell them he's seizing. Elias seized for thirty seconds and stopped. Then he had another seizure for thirty seconds and stopped. Next he kicked into this full-blown thing. They pulled him off the table and people were all going crazy and swarming the room, trying to get the seizure to stop. Fifteen minutes of seizing had gone by and they were pumping in a kitchen sink full of drugs as I watched, shaking, terrified. Then someone called the grief counselors for us and I went into full panic mode.

The respiratory guys were now in there bagging him, assisting his breathing. He was breathing on his own, but he had a lot of foam and they were suctioning it. And they just kept giving him all of these things.

I leaned down and talked to Elias. I tried my best to hold it together and kept saying to him, "Okay, honey, stop, Mommy's here, stop." And still they kept giving him stuff, but it just wasn't working.

I looked at the clock and thought, "Okay, it's been forty-five minutes," and I was screaming, "Do something! Come on! What's next?"

They were saying, "Okay, we're doing this, we're doing that." Then they hooked him up with phenobarbital. If that didn't work, they would have to put him in a coma. When they gave him the phenobarbital, his heart rate continued to be really really really high the whole time. Really high.

So they gave him the second phenobarbital to induce coma and we could see his seizures start to slow down. Then all of a sudden, his heart rate came flying down. The nurse shouted for Harry and me to get out! They literally shoved us out of the room. As we staggered out, we saw the crash cart being wheeled in.

I went numb. We could hear what they were saying

about his blood pressure and everything else because we were standing right outside the room. It was at that moment I had a feeling he wasn't going to make it.

We then heard them shout, "He went into cardiac arrest." Everyone began to frantically work to resuscitate him. I couldn't believe this was happening. They got him back, but then he crashed again, and they got him back, and he crashed again.

Harry and I stood outside the room in shock at what was unfolding in front of us. People were walking by staring at the room as they passed us as if they were all stopping to watch a car accident on the side of the road. It bothered me so much. I was in such pain.

I closed my eyes and thought, "He's gone now." I brought him in for a stupid sore throat, and here he is, having cardiac arrest. As I looked into the room, I saw a crush of people and could read the body language and the facial expressions. I looked at my husband and we both stood there numb. Then they got him back. They stabilized him.

But by the time they had rushed him up to ICU, they said he was no longer stable. They walked over to us and said, "Do you want to call anyone? We think it's time you started to call your family." The worst thing a mother can hear. I stood at his bedside and looked at my boy. He was on a respirator, and tubes were everywhere. All I could think was, "This can't be happening. This can't be happening."

The EEG results came back, and they told us Elias was

almost brain dead. They said their hope was that it was just the phenobarbital, which puts a body in a temporary coma, causing the almost flat line. So we should wait and see.

And so we waited and waited and just waited and he never moved. He couldn't hold his own blood pressure anymore so they started giving him all these blood pressure meds and had to keep upping the doses, because every time he'd start to fail, they would have to up the amount a little more, and a little more every time. Then he couldn't hold his own body temperature and had to have a heat blanket.

He didn't open his eyes, he didn't move, he couldn't pee. He wasn't putting out any urine, which was bad because it meant his kidneys were going. So they called a family conference and said, "Let's give it twenty-four hours and watch."

Then came the other most painful words a mother can ever hear... the nurse said, "And you might want to consider a Do Not Resuscitate." The world stopped. I didn't know what to do with myself. I couldn't take this much pain.

They said within twenty-four hours they were going to do a second EEG and see where he was, but if nothing changed, they were considering Elias brain-dead.

My husband made them bring in a TV so we could play all of his favorite videos, his favorite music, any books, just to try to stimulate anything.

One of the residents in the neurology department came in the next morning, and she was talking to him. "Hi, little guy." But he never moved. Then the nurse came in an hour later, checked him, and looked at me and said, "I wish we could do more."

That was when, if we had any hope at all, we lost it. She said, "They don't ever come out of this."

I looked at my boy with a million wires and tubes coming out of him and had them move them all so I could crawl up next to him. I held him for eight hours and I stayed with him until he died. I felt an energy pass through me that made my heart skip a beat. It was an orange energy. I knew it was Elias.

He was pronounced dead at 12:26. My husband, Harry, had pointed out to me the significance of that time. We believe all of this happened because of the vaccinations he received at his four-month wellness checkup. That date was the day after Christmas...12/26. Elias died at 12:26. On that vaccination day, my husband had joked to the doctor that Elias was given enough shots to kill an elephant. Instead, it killed a beautiful boy named Elias.

He will forever be in our hearts.

28

Guardian Angel

I LEFT MY INTERVIEW with Gina, holding back my tears, trying desperately to get back to my car. I felt heaviness in my chest that only a mother who had walked partway in her shoes could feel. I climbed into the front seat, closed the door, and screamed as loud as I possibly could. The pain. The pain. The pain. I screamed to let it all out. My chest had felt like a volcano waiting to erupt and I did just that. I cried so hard sitting on the side of the road. Playing back her story in my head, over and over, it crippled me. It tore me up, the suffering and loss of Gina's son. I also cried at the memory of an event that had taken place with Evan a couple of months ago and brought him almost to death.

Evan had come home from school with a tummy ache. This tummy ache was followed by vomiting. I knew it was going to be a long night so I hung in there with him, cleaning up the puke and carrying him back and forth from the bed to the toilet. He was vomiting more than I had ever seen with the stomach flu. He also had some diarrhea. Anytime I tried giving him a sip of water, he would vomit even more.

When the sun finally came up, Evan looked awful. He begged me for a sip of something, anything, and I kept turning him down, afraid that he would vomit again. Then around nine A.M. he asked to go into his room and lie down. He didn't want to lie on the couch with me anymore, which was unusual. I brought him into his room and lay down with him there. He started to babble and hallucinate. So I immediately shouted out to my dad, who was staying with me, "Dad, call 911!" I stripped off Evan's clothes to cool him down and brought him back into the living room. He continued to hallucinate and babble and I started screaming into his face to bring him back to reality. I didn't know what was going on. I had never seen this before. His pupils were dilated.

Finally, he said, "Mama," and I knew he was back. The paramedics arrived, whom we had gotten to know, and I told them we needed to go to the hospital because Evan could be having seizures. We loaded ourselves into the ambulance and went to the nearest hospital. Evan was talking to the paramedics and they were surprised at how well he was doing with his development. Of course, whether they liked it or not, I gave these guys my ten-minute lecture about clearing out toxins in the body. We arrived in the emergency room and they asked me questions and finally put us in an examination room.

Forty-five minutes had passed while we still waited for the doctor, and then it happened. Evan started convulsing in my arms. I ran his shaking body into the nurse's station, screaming, "He's having a seizure, do something!" The nurse yelled at me to put him down on the table. A male nurse came over and started to put an IV in Evan's arm. It takes a little longer than usual to get a needle into a child whose whole body is convulsing, and watching it feels like an eternity. I stood there watching this, saying to myself, "Not again! Not again." I prayed to God this would not be a bad one. Evan had gone into cardiac arrest before and I kept shouting that information to them so they would move faster.

Over a minute had gone by and the IV was in but no medicine was being given to stop the seizures. I kept yelling at the nurse, "Where the hell is the Ativan? Get the goddamn Ativan and make it stop."

He said, "It's coming, it's coming."

From where, Timbuktu? What the hell is taking so long?

I ran out of Evan's room and found a medicine closet with a nurse standing in it casually looking for something. I said, "Are you looking for the Ativan?"

"Yes," she said nonchalantly and kept looking, as though she was trying to find a book in a library.

I gave her all of ten more seconds until I started screaming at her. "Find the goddamn Ativan already! Get it! Let's go! Come on!"

She finally found it and two-stepped it into Evan's room. They loaded the syringe and injected it into his IV. And we waited. Thirty seconds went by and the seizure was not stopping. Another minute went by and the seizure was not stopping. Four more minutes went by and the seizure was still not stopping.

I shouted, "Come on, give him more! Please do something." They told me to calm down and injected him with more. Another two minutes went by and he was still seizing. He had been seizing for about ten minutes. Everyone was standing around the bed helplessly watching my little boy convulse.

It had now been twenty minutes and Evan was still seizing. They gave him a Tylenol suppository to lower his fever, and put ice packs all over his body. Now twenty-five minutes of seizing had gone by and he was shaking even harder because of the ice packs. I couldn't take it. I started shouting to Evan, "Come on, baby. Come on, Evan."

They injected more Ativan in him and I looked at the clock: thirty minutes of seizing. After another five minutes, I started screaming for fucking PLAN B because nothing seemed to be working. The head doctor called the pharmacy and ordered a bag of phenobarbital. In the meantime, they brought a crash cart into the room and my body went limp. The nurse looked at me and said, "Just in case, we want to be ready."

I was standing in hell. I didn't think I could physically handle the amount of pain I was experiencing.

The phenobarbital drip was now hooked up to Evan's IV and I had to watch each drip, hoping and praying that one of those drips would stop the seizure. Forty-five minutes had passed and he was still seizing. They had the crash unit standing by, respiratory machine people standing by, all waiting in case the worst happened.

All of a sudden, Evan's body stopped convulsing and he started snoring. I fell down to my knees and gave thanks to God that Evan didn't go into cardiac arrest. My dad was there and I looked back at his face and he looked as numb as I felt. Evan and my dad had become soul mates and I'm sure my dad's heart took as much of a beating as my own.

I looked back at Evan and gave him a kiss on the head. I took a big deep breath and prayed that the worst was over. Ten minutes later he started convulsing again. "NO! It's happening again!"

The nurses ran back to the room and said, "There is nothing more we can give him. We have to hope the phenobarbital kicks in more and makes it stop."

I leaned down to Evan's ear and started talking to him. "Stay with me, baby, stay with me, come back to Mama." Three more minutes and he stopped convulsing. My body went limp again. Please, God, no more.

And yet, one minute later, he started convulsing again. They gave him another Tylenol suppository and more ice packs. I watched the clock. Two more minutes of seizing and then he stopped again and began snoring.

This on-and-off seizing continued for three hours. The doctor came into the room and said we needed to get to a hospital with an intensive care unit, but we couldn't transfer him until he was stable.

Another hour went by and the seizures hadn't stopped. I was numb watching him. I was worried that when Evan came out of this, his brain would be a vegetable. I had thoughts of him dying here, and when that thought would play out in my head, it was usually followed by the thought of how I would kill myself the fastest possible way.

The doctor came into the room and told me they were going to give him another bag of phenobarbital to induce a coma. He said it was the next step to get the seizure to stop. I asked him how it worked and he said, "It makes the brain essentially go dead and completely shut down all activity." My heart almost stopped. He continued, "Usually we have to then take over his breathing for him because he won't be able to breathe for himself. He will be on a respirator." I felt my knees begin to shake and was about to pass out. He could tell I wasn't doing well, so he took me to another room and admitted me as a patient. My blood pressure was off the charts. After they gave me an Ativan, I ran back to join Evan. They had started the other phenobarbital bag and I knew he was slowly drifting into a coma.

Evan finally stopped seizing after six hours. The paramedic team came in to transfer us to a pediatric intensive care unit. I was scared to move him because I was afraid of stirring him into another seizure. They assured me the likelihood of that was slim. Evan was in a coma.

Riding in the ambulance, I stared at the oxygen intake number on the beep-beep machine. They had not put him on a respirator yet and only needed to provide an oxygen mask. As long as his oxygen intake was good, they wouldn't need the respirator, so I prayed that my little boy would be able to keep those lungs moving.

The neurologist met us at the new hospital and looked into Evan's eyes. "Wow, he is in a heavy coma." She looked at how many drugs they gave him within that six-hour period and was blown away. That night, I curled up next to Evan and prayed that things would start getting better.

The next morning, Evan had of course not moved at all. He was still not on a respirator and they were surprised that he was managing his own breathing. They looked at his pupils and said, "He's still out." I asked, For how long? They told me it just depends on how fast his liver can move the phenobarbital out of his system. I sat next to him all day, singing him songs and telling him how much I love him.

At day three, Evan was still in a coma. He had not moved at all. I noticed that he started to look worse. He was very, very pale. The nurse had come into the room and listened to his lungs and they sounded wet. He started to sound wheezy. She left the room and a half hour later they brought in an X-ray machine. I asked them what this was for and they said they were checking for pneumonia. By now, I was emotionally exhausted. I almost passed out again. I was physically shaking and ready to scream to the heavens, "Enough already!"

The X-ray came back clear. Thank you, God. Thank you, God.

Later that night, the nurse came in and said, "He's looking a little blue." She was right. I was so used to staring at him every second of the day, I didn't see how blue he had gotten. She looked up at the oxygen intake and it was really, really low. She said to me, "He's having trouble moving his lungs. He's going to need to go on a respirator if he doesn't start taking bigger breaths in the next hour."

She walked out of the room and I burst into tears. We had come so far. To have him go on a respirator now was not an option for me. I climbed on top of his bed and stood over his body. I bent over and got right into Evan's face and started screaming at the top of my lungs.

"EVAN, IT'S TIME TO WAKE UP NOW. YOU'VE GOT TO COME BACK NOW. I NEED YOU TO BREATHE, BABY. I NEED YOU TO BREATHE. WAKE UP, BABY. COME OUT OF THIS. I WANNA GO PLAY NOW, OKAY? BREATHE, BABY, BREATHE." I was screaming so loud that the entire floor of the hospital could hear me.

I screamed as loud as I could for a full hour, staring at that oxygen number. The nurse came back into the room and saw me on top of him, yelling at him to wake up. She walked over to the machine and checked the number. She smiled, looked at me, and said, "You did it. Whatever you did just worked. Look." I looked up at the machine and his breathing number had doubled. The nurse patted me on the back and said, "Good job, Mom. You really did it." I climbed off the bed and burst into tears. I sat in the corner of the floor begging for some relief.

The next day, Evan started moaning. I jumped up and started yelling again. "Baby, I can hear you. It's Mama. Can you open your eyes?" The nurses came back in the room and started poking him everywhere to get a response. He was responding! He was flinching. I was so excited he was coming out of his coma. I was so grateful he was back. I didn't know what his brain was going to be like but I held on tight to the vision of him saying "Mama." I continued to sing to him and stimulate him, and my sister, who is Evan's other soul mate, came to visit. I started yelling, "Jojo is here, Evan!"

He slowly opened an eye, even though it was rolling back in his head, and he slurred, "No...Jojo." I started screaming and jumping up and down. I ran out to the nurse's station and said, "He said something. He said something." The amazing thing about "No Jojo" is that it's a joke we play with Evan. Whenever Jojo comes over, I say, "Jojo is here," and Evan pretends that he doesn't want her and says, "No Jojo. I only want Mama," and then they tickle each other. The fact that he said "No Jojo" was so huge because it was part of our joke. It meant that he understood.

Hours had passed and Evan started to open his eyes even more. He was still so incredibly sedated that any couple of words he said sounded like a drunken sailor or a brain-injured person. I was hoping not the latter.

Day five in the hospital and Evan was awake but very groggy. He could barely speak, but he was more alert. Sadly, he started vomiting again and had explosive diarrhea. It turned out he had caught the rotavirus from school. (Gee, I'm so glad that vaccine the doctor gave him to stave off the rotavirus worked.) I felt bad that he was coming out of a coma and having to deal with more puking, no food, and not being able to say more than three slurred words.

When we were finally released from the hospital, we went home and I dragged my mattress onto the floor. He was still unable to walk and I was worried he would roll off the bed. I lay next to him on this bed for weeks. It took a full month for Evan to regain his speech and ability to walk. I was worried he would have damage to his brain, but a full month later he regained everything.

It was at this point, when I knew he was in the clear, that I fell into a depression. I was physically and emotionally drained, walking around like a zombie. I was so frightened of Evan getting sick that I didn't think I was ever going to let him out of the house again. I knew I had to get past the emotional crippling I was experiencing, but the fear of losing him was too great. Truthfully, it haunts me every day.

As I sat in the car recalling this, I prayed to Gina's little boy, Elias, who hadn't pulled through this same experience. I told him his death would never be forgotten and that his story would be shared with the world to help make change. I told Elias he was going to be part of this change. I also asked him to be Evan's guardian angel, to look over my boy so we could both continue to send our message loud and clear to the rest of the world.

29

Collective Awakening

IF THERE WAS EVER A NEED for a call to action to mothers around the world, the time is right now. What's going on in the world can no longer be overlooked or discredited. People can say there is no science to support our beliefs about the causes of autism and ways to treat it, but there is plenty of evidence. Just walk into the homes of families who have children with autism. They'll be happy to introduce you to their science.

When did people become so trusting of government organizations or even paramedical companies? Sooner or later, many of these organizations become corrupt. It's inevitable. Remember when they told us smoking was good for our health? Remember they told us autism was because of emotionally cold and lazy mothers? How many times have medications come on the market, deemed safe, and then pulled off the market owing to major side effects? Are we to believe that ALL thirty-six vaccinations given now are ALL safe with no side effects? Give me a break. Are we supposed to buy the fact that these shots are one-size-fits-all? Or that every child is born with a perfect immune system? Wake the hell up, America, and think hard about the logic in this.

In the meantime, I hope mothers across America will join me in our fight to change this insane vaccine schedule and demand that they GREEN our vaccines. Take the crap out! Enough is enough.

These kids are here for a reason, a much bigger purpose than we are all probably even aware of. They are showing us we need to make some major changes in this world and we need to care for our bodies and for this planet. We have to listen to the message they bring and assist them in every possible way we can. They are the messengers and we are the doers. So let's start *doing* something about it.

30

A Mother Warrior Is . . .

A MOTHER WHO HEARS there is no hope for her child and, instead of retreating and mourning, breaks down walls, weaves her way through obstacles, follows her intuition even when people tell her she is crazy. She is a mother who believes in hope. A mother who believes in miracles and is able to carry on with strength and determination, even when her partner doubts her and offers no support. A mother who never gives up when she keeps hitting dead ends. These are the women who will continue to open the door so future generations of children don't have to suffer. These are the mothers with hearts of gold and shields made of the strongest armor.

I know in my heart that someday this era will be marked as an era when a group of parents fought the giants to help save their babies and future generations. Margaret Mead, the late great sociologist, once said, "Never doubt that a small group of thoughtful committed citizens can change the world; indeed, it's the only thing that ever has."

These are the women I walk beside proudly and whose numbers I hope will grow. We are the seekers of change. We are the seekers of truth. We are the Mother Warriors and we will never give up.

Generation Rescue

Jenny McCarthy's Autism Organization

Generation Rescue is a parent-run charitable organization
that supports and educates families in need
and funds leading scientific research.

FOR MORE INFORMATION ON
Diets
Alternative vaccine schedules
Biomedical therapies

log on to generationrescue.org.

TALK TO A RESCUE ANGEL

You can talk one-on-one with a mom who has gone through
biomedical interventions with her own child by finding a
Rescue Angel on generationrescue.org.

Resources

Kirkman Laboratories
Get all the nutritional supplements
your child needs.
1-800-245-8282
www.kirkmanlabs.com

Mona Vie
The health benefits of acai have been
validated by modern science. This
superfood contains antioxidants,
amino acids, vitamins,
phytonutrients, and trace minerals.
The popular choice among families
who have children with autism has
been The Original.
For more information, go to www.
thegreatproduct.com/jojo.

**Methyl B12 (MB12) Dissolvable
Strips**
MB12 without a prescription,
developed by Stan Kurtz
www.mb12strips.org

Infrared Sauna
Heavenly Heat
To order, call 1-800-697-2862 (1-800
My Sauna).
For Parent/Child brochures, e-mail
bobmorgan@heavenlyheat
saunas.com.

**Hyperbaric Oxygen Chambers
Oxy Health LLC**
1-877-789-0123
information@oxyhealth.com
www.oxyhealth.com

Children's Corner School
Focused on children ages two to six,
some with conditions such as autism,
ADHD, and chronic illness. The
individualized approach includes
special diets, supplementation, and a
Green School Environment as a
foundation for prevention,
development, and recovery.

Van Nuys, California
information@childrenscorner
school.com
www.childrenscornerschool.com

Educational DVDs
Teach2Talk
Teach2Talk, LLC, produces
educational resources for children
which target core speech and
language, play, and social skills using
techniques including video modeling.
www.teach2talk.com

DAN! Doctor Directory

The following are practitioners listed by the Autism Research Institute as providing Defeat Autism Now!® interventions for patients with autism. Most are physicians; others are licensed health care professionals in related fields.

The Autism Research Institute has no means of certifying the competence or quality of practice of any practitioner. The lists are provided as a community service. The Autism Research Institute disclaims and does not endorse or support any individual or entity listed; makes no representations, warranties, guarantees, or promises on behalf of or for those listed; and assumes no liability or responsibility for any service or product provided. *ARI does not certify practitioners or guarantee competence, skill, knowledge, or experience.* Please continually check the Autism Research Institute for updated lists.

Alaska

Adam Grove, N.D.
3330 Eagle Street
Anchorage, AK 99503
ph: 907-561-2330
fax: 907-561-1280

Arizona

Matthew Baral, N.D.
International Child Development
Resource Center
1620 N. 48th Street
Phoenix, AZ 85008
ph: 321-259-7111

Eli Ber, N.M.D.
10752 N. 89th Place B213
Scottsdale, AZ 85260
ph: 480-634-6172
fax: 480-634-6975

Martha M. Grout, M.D., M.D.H.
The Cross Roads Clinic
9328 E. Raintree Drive
Scottsdale, AZ 85260
ph: 480-240-2600
fax: 480-240-2601

Alan K. Ketover, M.D., M.D.H.
The Valley Clinic
10595 N. Tatum Boulevard, Suite E-146
Paradise Valley, AZ 85253
ph: 602-381-0800
fax: 602-381-0054

Allen Lewis, M.D., F.A.A.P.
Pfeiffer Treatment Center
4575 Weaver Parkway
Warrenville, IL 60555
outreach clinics in AZ
ph: 866-504-6076 (toll free)

Joel Morgan, N.M.D.
Total Wellness Medical Center
9887 West Bell Road
Sun City, AZ 85351
ph: 623-977-0077
fax: 623-977-0057

Geoffrey P. Radoff, M.D., M.D.H.
Alternative Medical Care of AZ
2525 West Greenway Road, Suite 210
Phoenix, AZ 85023
ph: 702-755-6475
fax: 602-993-0207

Cindy Schneider, M.D.
Center for Autism Research and Education
300 E. Osborn Road #200
Phoenix, AZ 85012
ph: 602-277-2273
fax: 602-277-2283

Maureen Schwehr, N.D.
Body Balance Natural Health Clinic
1151 S. La Canada, Suite 103
Green Valley, AZ 85614
ph: 520-399-9499
fax: 820-742-3846

Arkansas

Betsy Hendricks, M.D.
2425 Prince Street, Suite 3
Conway, AR 72034
ph: 501-327-2967
fax: 501-327-7866

Stephen Kahler, M.D.
Arkansas Children's Hospital
800 Marshall Street, Slot 512-22
Little Rock, AR 72202
ph: 501-364-2966
fax: 501-364-2964

California

Thauna Abrin, N.D.
45 Quail Court, Suite 200
Walnut Creek, CA 94596
ph: 510-282-2104
fax: 510-228-0338

Koren Barrett, N.D.
California Integrative Hyperbaric
Center (CIHC)
16251 Laguna Canyon Road,
Suite 175
Irvine, CA 92618
ph: 949-428-8878
fax: 949-428-8874

Chitra Bhakta, M.D.
Tustin Medical Plaza
14591 Newport Avenue, Suite 208
Tustin, CA 92780
ph: 949-474-2144
fax: 949-242-2536

*James Blumenthal, D.C., C.C.N.,
D.A.C.B.N.*
2211 Corinth Avenue, Suite 310
Los Angeles, CA 90064
ph: 310-445-3350
fax: 310-445-3351

*Shawn K. Centers, D.O., F.A.C.O.P.,
M.H.*
Osteopathic Center for Children
4135 54th Place
San Diego, CA 92105
ph: 619-583-7611
fax: 619-583-0296

Terrance Chang, M.D.
8723 Sierra College Boulevard,
Suite 220
Roseville, CA 95746
ph: 916-791-0797

Victoria Cupic, M.D.
Institute for Progressive Medicine
4 Hughes, Suite 175
Irvine, CA 92618
ph: 949-600-5100

Shivinder S. Deol
4000 Stockdale Highway, Suite D
Bakersfield, CA 93309
ph: 661-325-7452
fax: 661-325-7456

Robin Eckert, M.D.
Laguna Center for Integrative
Medicine
105 Crescent Bay Drive #D
Laguna Beach, CA 92651
ph: 949-725-0000
fax: 949-494-9683

Donald Gerken, D.C.
88 E. Bonita Road, Suite E
Chula Vista, CA 91910
ph: 619-422-3088
fax: 619-422-3988

David Getoff, N.D., C.C.N., C.N.C.
11819 Via Granero
El Cajon, CA 92019
ph: 619-468-6846

Julie Griffith, M.D., M.S., C.M.T.
Northern California Center for
Learning & Behavioral Disorders
120 Ross Valley Drive
San Rafael, CA 94901
ph: 415-925-1616
fax: 415-259-4011

Karima Hirani, M.D.
9736 Venice Boulevard
Culver City, CA 90232
ph: 310-559-6634
fax: 310-559-6652

Miriam Jang, M.D.
528 Biscayne Dr.
San Rafael, CA 94901
ph: 415-457-3193
fax: 415-459-2293

Toril H. Jelter, M.D.
460 Marshall Drive
Walnut Creek, CA 94598
ph: 925-788-8904
fax: 925-947-1075

Richard Kunin, M.D.
2698 Pacific Avenue
San Francisco, CA 94115
ph: 415-346-2500
fax: 415-346-2519

Allen Lewis, M.D., F.A.A.P.
Pfeiffer Treatment Center
4575 Weaver Parkway
Warrenville, IL 60555
outreach clinics in CA
ph: 866-504-6076 (toll free)

Thomas Lin, M.D.
4634 Barranca Parkway
Irvine, CA 92604
ph: 949-387-2818
fax: 949-654-7668

Cathie Lippman, M.D.
291 S. La Cienga Boulevard,
Suite 207
Beverly Hills, CA 90211
ph: 310-289-8430
fax: 310-289-8165

Joel Lopez, M.D.
Synergy Medical of San Francisco
1500 Taylor Street
San Francisco, CA 94133
ph: 415-567-5602
fax: 415-358-4456

Luc Maes, D.C., N.D.
9 E. Mission Street
Santa Barbara, CA 93101
ph: 805-563-8660
fax: 805-563-8662

Nicola McFadzean, N.D.
1111 Fort Stockton Drive, Suite H
San Diego, CA 92103
ph: 619-546-4065
fax: 619-270-2582

Lynne Mielke, M.D.
Developmental Spectrums
4463 Stoneridge Drive, Suites A & C
Pleasanton, CA 94588
ph: 925-846-6300
fax: 925-846-6323

Rochelle Neally, D.C.
3645 E. 4th Street "B"
Long Beach, CA 90814
ph: 562-987-5507
fax: 562-987-5506

Gina L. Nick, N.M.D.
265 Laguna Avenue
Laguna Beach, CA 92651
ph: 800-439-1382
fax: 800-439-1382

Raj Patel, M.D.
5050 El Camino Real, Suite 110
Los Altos, CA 94022
ph: 650-964-6700
fax: 650-964-3549

Geoffrey P. Radoff, M.D., M.D.H.
Trinity Autism Center of San Diego
7907 Ostrow Street
San Diego, CA 92111
ph: 858-926-8366

Geoffrey Saft, D.C.
California Hyperbaric Oxygen
Therapy
21 Tamal Vista Boulevard, Suite 210
Corte Madera, CA 94925
ph: 415-927-8828

Susan Schmidt-Lackner, M.D.
3200 Motor Avenue
Los Angeles, CA 90034
ph: 310-836-1223 ext 379
fax: 310-204-4134

Hitendra Shah, M.D.
23341 Golden Springs #210
Diamond Bar, CA 91765
ph: 909-860-2610
fax: 909-860-1192

Eric Sletten, M.D.
64 N. Brent Street, Suite A
Ventura, CA 93003
ph: 805-643-7902
fax: 805-643-7863

Elisa Song, M.D.
1601 El Camino Real, Suite 101
Belmont, CA 94002
ph: 650-595-5437
fax: 650-595-5438

Allan Sosin, M.D.
Institute for Progressive Medicine
4 Hughes, Suite 175
Irvine, CA 92618
ph: 949-600-5100
fax: 949-600-5101

Ursula Stehle, Ph.D.
4112 Pennsylvania Avenue
Fair Oaks, CA 95628
ph: 916-962-0222
fax: 916-962-1055

Kenneth P. Stoller, M.D.
1936 Stockston Avenue
Sacramento, CA 95816
ph: 505-955-8560 / 916-732-9030

Denise A. Tarasuk, R.N., N.D.
51 E. Campbell Avenue, Suite 101F
Campbell, CA 95008
ph: 408-370-5291
fax: 408-370-5293

David Traver, M.D.
1261 E. Hillsdale Boulevard
Foster City, CA 94404
ph: 650-341-5300
fax: 650-341-5900

John Toth, D.O.
2270 Bacon Street
Concord, CA 94520
ph: 925-687-9447
fax: 925-687-9483

Suzann Wang, N.D.
616 University Avenue
Palo Alto, CA 9411
ph: 415-331-1823
fax: 650-331-7250

Rachel West, D.O.
318 S. Lincoln Avenue, #225
Venice, CA 90291
ph: 310-450-8959
fax: 310-396-3645

Kurt Norman Woeller, D.O.
Stillpoint Center Integrative Med.
Vail Ranch Towne Square
32605 Temecula Parkway / 79 South,
Suite 201
Temecula, CA 92592
ph: 951-693-2267
fax: 951-693-2268

Ann Wolf, M.D.
1601 El Camino Real, Suite 101
Belmont, CA 94001
ph: 650-595-5437

Colorado

Michael Catalano, M.D.
2801 Youngfield Street, Suite 117
Lakewood, CO 80401
ph: 303-233-4247
fax: 303-233-4249

Deborah Hamilton, M.D.
Holistic Pediatric Consulting
1800 30th Street, Suite 304
Boulder, CO 80301
ph: 303-442-0107
fax: 303-442-3317

John Kucera, M.D.
6475 Wall Street, Suite 100
Colorado Springs, CO 80908
ph: 719-596-1118
fax: 719-573-9774

Steve Parcell, N.D.
5330 Manhattan Circle
Boulder, CO 80303
ph: 303-884-7557
fax: 303-448-9069

Connecticut

Eileen Comia, M.D.
Avon Therapeutic Center for
Children, LLC
701 Cottage Grove Road, Suite C-010
Bloomfield, CT 06002
ph: 860-242-2200
fax: 860-242-2212

Richard Cooper, N.D.
72 Park Street, Suite 105
New Canaan, CT 06840
ph: 203-972-6800
fax: 203-972-6820

Brain Henninger, N.D.
The Brickwalk
1275 Post Road, Suite A-19
Fairfield, CT 06824
ph: 203-255-4325
fax: 203-254-7340

Victoria Kobliner, M.S., R.D., CD-N
150 Danbury Road
Wilton, CT 06897
ph: 203-834-2813
fax: 203-834-2831

Nancy O'Hara, M.D.
150 Danbury Road
Wilton, CT 06897
ph: 203-834-2813
fax: 203-834-2831

James S. Sensenig, N.D.
2558 Whitney Avenue
Hamden, CT 06518
ph: 203-230-2200
fax: 203-230-1454

Fran Storch, N.D.
203 Storrs Road
P.O. Box 406
Mansfield Center, CT 06250
ph: 860-423-2759
fax: 860-423-9676

Gail Szakacs, M.D.
150 Danbury Road
Wilton, CT 06897
ph: 203-834-2813
fax: 203-834-2831

Lynn Williamson, R.N., M.S.
45 Notch Road
Bolton, CT 06043
ph: 860-649-9129
fax: 860-643-2762

Victoria Zupa, N.D.
397 Post Road
Darien, CT 06820
ph: 203-656-4300
fax: 203-656-1444

Washington, DC

Charlene Kannankeril, N.D.
5225 Wisconsin Avenue, NW,
Suite 401
Washington, DC 20015
ph: 202-237-7000 Ext. 120
fax: 202-237-0017

*George Mitchell, M.D., with Julie
Leonard, P.A.C.*
2639 Connecticut Avenue,
NW, #C-100
Washington, DC 20008
ph: 202-265-4111
fax: 202-265-1907

Florida

David Berger, M.D.
Wholistic Pediatrics
3341 West Bearss Avenue
Tampa, FL 33618
ph: 813-960-3415
fax: 813-960-3465

Katherine Clements, N.D.
Aurora Therapeutics, Inc.
3131 S. Tamiami Trail, Suite 206
Sarasota, FL 34239
ph: 941-951-6820
fax: 941-951-6821

*Charlotte Fudge, R.N., M.S.N.,
B.C.B.A.*
Butterfly Effects, LLC
2708 NE 14th Street, Suite 5
Pompano Beach, FL 33062
ph: East Coast Office:
954-603-7885
fax: 954-342-0273
ph: West Coast Office:
941-306-3873

Patricia Jenkins, R.N., Ph.D.
Butterfly Effects, LLC
2708 NE 14th Street, Suite 5
Pompano Beach, FL 33062
ph: East Coast Office: 954-603-7885
fax: 954-342-0273
ph: West Coast Office: 941-306-3873

Jerrold J. Kartzinel, M.D.
5270 Palm Valley Road
Ponte Vedra Beach, FL 32082
ph: 904-543-1288
fax: 904-543-1289

Andrew Levinson, M.D.
410 Meridian Avenue
Miami Beach, FL 33139
ph: 305-466-1100
fax: 305-466-1160

Lisa Marsh, D.C.
1114 Florida Avenue, Suite C
Palm Harbor, FL 34683
ph: 727-772-1966
fax: 727-772-0096

Frank Maye, D.O.M., N.M.D.
7800 SW 57th Avenue, Suite 126
Miami, FL 33143
ph: 305-668-9555
fax: 786-533-2399

Courtnee L Pingaro, D.C.
12401 Orange Drive #219
Davie, FL 33330
ph: 954-862-1430
fax: 954-862-1431

Lisa R. Ramey, D.O.
30 Windsormere Way, Suite 100
Oviedo, FL 32765
ph: 407-359-1770
fax: 407-971-4264

Dan Rossignol, M.D.
International Child Development
Resource Center
3800 W. Eau Gallie Boulevard,
Suite 105
Melbourne, FL 32934
ph: 321-259-7111
fax: 321-259-7222

Andrea Schaeffer-Pautz, M.D.
Persephone Healing Arts Center
485 Sixth Avenue North
Jacksonville Beach, FL 32250
ph: 904-246-3583
fax: 904-246-3778

Albert Zant, M.D.
913 MarWalt Drive
Fort Walton Beach, FL 32547
ph: 850-243-8229
fax: 850-863-2540

Georgia

Linda Nathanson-Lippitt, M.D.
2400 Herodian Way, Suite 150
Smyrna, GA 30080
ph: 770-850-8588
fax: 770-850-8789

Anthony Neary, D.C.
4080 McGinnis Ferry Road, Building
300, Suite 302
Alpharetta, GA 30005
ph: 678-992-1920
fax: 770-410-9510

Marilyn Peterson, D.C.
2519 Parkwood Road
Snellville, GA 30039
ph: 678-344-6821

Hank M. Sloan, N.M.D.
Genesis Health Center
104 Colony Park Drive, Suite 800
Cumming, GA 30040
ph: 678-947-4454
fax: 678-208-9876

Illinois

Alan Bain, D.O.
55 E. Washington Street, Suite 3305
Chicago, IL 60602
ph: 312-236-7010
fax: 312-236-7190

Georgia Davis, M.D.
1112 Rickard Road
Springfield, IL 62704
ph: 217-787-9540
fax: 217-787-9183

W. Robert Elghammer, M.D.
723 N. Logan
Danville, IL 61832
ph: 217-446-3259
fax: 217-446-0242

Patty Fallon, R.N.
True Health Medical Center
603 E. Diehl Road, #135
Naperville, IL 60563
ph: 630-505-4040
fax: 630-505-9847

Sonja M. Hintz, R.N.
603 East Diehl Road
Naperville, IL 60563
ph: 630-505-4040
fax: 630-505-9847

Elena Koles, M.D., Ph.D.
666 Dundee Road, #602
Northbrook, IL 60062
ph: 847-291-0900
fax: 847-291-9344

Allen T. Lewis, M.D., F.A.A.P.
Pfeiffer Treatment Center
4575 Weaver Parkway
Warrenville, IL 60555
ph: 630-505-0300
fax: 630-836-0667

Jane Reinhardt-Martin, R.D.
The Integrative Wellness Center
2526 41st Street
Moline, IL 61265
ph: 309-792-7107
fax: 309-764-9326

Anju Usman, M.D.
True Health Medical Center
603 E. Diehl Road, # 135
Naperville, IL 60563
ph: 630-505-4040
fax: 630-505-9847

Tracy Ziemann, P.A.-C.
True Health Medical Center
603 E. Diehl Road, #135
Naperville, IL 60563
ph: 630-505-4040
fax: 630-505-9847

Indiana

Mary Lou Hulseman, M.D.
Fall Creek Family Medicine
9560 E. 59th Street
Indianapolis, IN 46216
ph: 317-621-1700
fax: 317-621-1711

Stacie Macari, D.C., C.N.S., D.A.B.A.A.H.P.
Carmel Clinic for Functional
Medicine
75 Executive Drive
Carmel, IN 46032
ph: 317-846-9335
fax: 317-846-8481

Rhonda J. Marsh, R.N.
Integrative Health Specialists of
Indiana
9333 N. Meridian Street, Suite 202
Indianapolis, IN 46260
ph: 317-580-9333
fax: 317-818-8933

Iowa

Carolyn R. Walker, M.S.N., B.S.N.
Prevention & Healing of Iowa
6901 Hickman Road
Urbandale, IA 50322
ph: 515-727-4141
fax: 515-727-4848

Kansas

Jeremy Baptist, M.D., Ph.D.
Allergy Link
6806 West 83rd Street
Overland Park, KS 66204
ph: 913-469-4043
fax: 913-469-6580

Michael Brown, N.M.D.
11240 Strang Line Road
Lenexa, KS 66215
ph: 913-498-0005
fax: 913-469-8688

Louisiana

Stephanie Cave, M.D.
10562 S. Glenstone Way
Baton Rouge, LA 70810
ph: 225-767-7433
fax: 225-767-4641

Maine

Patrick Mulcahy, D.D.S., D.O.
69 York Street, Suite 4
Kennebunk, ME 04043
ph: 207-985-3079
fax: 207-985-3775

Jane Robertson, D.C.
326 Belmont Avenue
Belfast, ME 04915
ph: 207-338-2024
fax: 207-338-9900

Fredric Shotz, N.D.
222 Auburn Street
Portland, ME 04103
ph: 207-828-4299
fax: 207-828-5056

Maryland

Arnold Brenner, M.D.
5400 Old Court Road, Suite 105
Randallstown, MD 21133
ph: 410-922-1133
fax: 410-922-9740

Laura R. Chaffiotte, D.C., C.C.N., D.A.C.B.A.
812 Tollhouse Avenue
Frederick, MD 21701
ph: 301-694-7774
fax: 301-694-9396

Pamela Compart, M.D.
Heart Light Healing Arts, Inc.
9145 Guilford Road, Suite 100
Columbia, MD 21046
ph: 410-880-4215
fax: 410-880-4192

Dana Laake, M.S., L.N.
Dana Laake Nutrition
11224 Orleans Way
Kensington, MD 20895
ph: 301-942-5505
fax: 301-942-5506

Richard E. Layton, M.D.
Dulaney Center II
901 Dulaney Valley Road, #101
Towson, MD 21204
ph: 410-337-2707
fax: 410-337-2841

Allen Lewis, M.D., F.A.A.P.
Pfeiffer Treatment Center
4575 Weaver Parkway
Warrenville, IL 60555
outreach clinics in MD
ph: 866-504-6076 (toll free)

Janelle Love, M.D.
1300 Ritchie Highway, Suite B
Arnold, MD 21012
ph: 410-544-8141
fax: 410-544-8143

Massachusetts

Carol Englender, M.D.
160 Speen Street, Suite 203
Framingham, MA 01701
ph: 508-875-0875
fax: 508-875-0005

Paul Millard Hardy, M.D.
Hardy Healthcare Associates
62 Derby Street
Hingham, MA 02043
ph: 781-740-8300
fax: 781-740-8242

Jeanne Hubbuch, M.D.
288 Walnut Street, Suite 420
Newton, MA 02460
ph: 617-965-7770
fax: 617-965-7378

Christine M. Keenan, R.N., M.S., C.N.S.
41 Church Street
Westfield, MA 01085
ph: 413-562-8200
fax: 413-562-5006

Nancy O'Hara, M.D.
377 Main Street
Wakefield, MA 01880
ph: 203-834-2813
fax: 203-834-2831

Gail Szakacs, M.D.
377 Main Street
Wakefield, MA 01880
ph: 203-834-2813
fax: 203-834-2831

Michigan

Robert DeJonge, D.O.
2251 E. Paris Avenue
Grand Rapids, MI 49546
ph: 616-956-6090
fax: 616-956-6099

Mark Leventer, M.D.
12337 E. Michigan
Grass Lake, MI 49240
ph: 517-522-8403
fax: 517-522-4275

Allen Lewis, M.D., F.A.A.P.
Pfeiffer Treatment Center
4575 Weaver Parkway
Warrenville, IL 60555, MI
ph: 866-504-6076 (toll free)

Richard Linsk, M.D., Ph.D.
1310 South Main Street
Ann Arbor, MI 48103
ph: 734-786-3833
fax: 734-786-3835

James R. Neuenschwander, M.D.
Bio Energy Medical Center
412 Longshore
Ann Arbor, MI 48105
ph: 734-995-3200
fax: 734-995-4254

Julie Stevens, D.O.
4676 E. Broomfield
Mt. Pleasant, MI 48858
ph: 989-772-7600
fax: 877-818-8934

Minnesota

Richard Mayfield, D.C., C.C.N.
7901 Xerxes Avenue South #300
Bloomington, MN 55431
ph: 952-885-0822
fax: 952-885-9180

Greg Mongeon, D.C.
1525 London Road
Duluth, MN 55812
ph: 218-722-4845
fax: 218-722-8480

Rachel Oppitz, N.D.
Itasca Naturopathic Clinic
17261 State 34
Park Rapids, MN 56470
ph: 218-237-2312
fax: 218-237-2311

Sandra Spore, R.N., D.C., N.M.D.
1530 W. Frontage Road
Stillwater, MN 55082
ph: 651-439-1013
fax: 651-439-3465

Kevin Wand, D.O.
Midwest Wellness Center
10562 France Avenue South
Bloomington, MN 55431
ph: 952-942-9303
fax: 952-252-0603

Missouri

Amy Davis, M.D.
16216 Baxter Road, Suite 110
Chesterfield, MO 63017
ph: 636-778-9158
fax: 636-778-9162

Neil J. Nathan, M.D.
2828 N. National Avenue, Suite D
Springfield, MO 65803
ph: 417-869-7583
fax: 417-869-7592

Alain Salas, D.C.
Pain and Stress Elimination Center
405 East 19th Avenue, Suite 205
North Kansas City, MO 64116
ph: 816-842-7246
fax: 816-842-7246

James D. Smith, D.C.
1802 N. Woodbine
St. Joseph, MO 64506
ph: 816-232-5113
fax: 816-232-0453

Tipu Sultan, M.D.
Environmental Health & Allergy
11585 West Florissant Avenue
Florissant, MO 63033
ph: 314-921-5600
fax: 314-921-8273

James Willoughby, D.O.
24 South Main Street
Liberty, MO 64068
ph: 816-781-0902
fax: 816-781-2562

Montana

Margaret Beeson, N.D.
Yellowstone Naturopathic Clinic
720 North 30th Street
Billings, MT 59101
ph: 406-259-5096
fax: 406-248-5655

Nebraska

LeAnn Jons-Cox, D.O.
Cornerstone Progressive Health
8031 W. Center Road, Suite 221
Omaha, NE 68124
ph: 402-343-7963
fax: 402-343-1330

Nevada

Geoffrey P. Radoff, M.D., M.D.H.
4760 S. Pecos Boulevard
Las Vegas, NV 89121
ph: 702-755-6475

New Hampshire

Lynn Durand, M.D.
81 Hall Street
Concord, NH 03301
ph: 603-228-7245
fax: 603-228-7406

Luke Huber, N.D.
95 Stiles Road, Suite 107
Salem, NH 03079
ph: 603-890-9900
fax: 603-890-9933

New Jersey

Peta Cohen, M.S., R.D.
Total Life Center
11 North Dean Street
Englewood, NJ 07631
ph: 201-541-7601
fax: 201-541-7876

Hui Ling Lynne Deng, M.D.
500 E. Camden Avenue, A-4
Moorestown, NJ 08057
ph: 856-722-1484
fax: 856-985-2866

David Dornfeld, D.O.
1680 State Highway 35
Middletown, NJ 07748
ph: 732-671-3730
fax: 732-706-1078

Stuart H. Freedenfeld, M.D.
56 South Main Street,
Suites A & B
Stockton, NJ 08559
ph: 609-397-8585
fax: 609-397-9335

John Gregg, D.O.
1083 Goffle Road
Hawthorne, NJ 07506
ph: 973-423-6060
fax: 973-423-1153

Kimberly Hamada, R.N.
56 South Main Street
Stockton, NJ 08559
ph: 609-397-8585
fax: 609-397-9335

*Elaine Hardy, M.S.,
R.N., A.P.N.*
Holistic Family Healthcare, PC
319 Airport Road
Hackettstown, NJ 07840
ph: 908-850-0888
fax: 908-850-1005

Allan Magaziner, D.O.
Magaziner Center for Wellness
1907 Greentree Road
Cherry Hill, NJ 08003
ph: 856-424-8222
fax: 856-424-2599

James Neubrander, M.D., F.A.A.E.M.
100 Menlo Park, Suite 410
Edison, NJ 08837
ph: 732-906-9000
fax: 732-906-9015

*Wendy Skiba-King, B.S.N., M.S.,
Ph.D.*
53 Kossuth Street, 1st Floor
Somerset, NJ 08873
ph: 973-218-9191
fax: 973-218-1199

New Mexico

Kenneth Stoller, M.D.
404 Brunn School Road #D
Santa Fe, NM 87505
ph: 505-955-8560 / 916-732-9030
fax: 916-732-9033

New York

Sidney M. Baker, M.D.
71 Ferry Road
Sag Harbor, NY 11963
ph: 631-725-9548
fax: 631-725-9549

Kenneth Bock, M.D.
108 Montgomery Street
Rhinebeck, NY 12572
ph: 845-876-7082
fax: 845-876-4615

Marvin Boris, M.D.
Allergy and Immunology (www.
AutismNY.com)
77 Froehlich Farm Boulevard
Woodbury, NY 11797
ph: 516-921-3456
fax: 516-364-1844

Geri Brewster, R.D., M.P.H., C.D.N.
14 Smith Avenue (rear office)
Mt. Kisco, NY 10549
ph: 914-864-1976
fax: 914-864-1967

Christopher Calapai, D.O.
1900 Hempstead Turnpike, Suite 503
East Meadow, NY 11554
ph: 516-794-0404
fax: 516-794-0332

Keri Chiappino, D.C., D.A.C.N.B.
50 West 72nd Street, Suite C-5
New York, NY 10023
ph: 212-721-1188

Keri Chiappino, D.C., D.A.C.N.B.
323 Middle Country Road,
Suite 1
Smithtown, NY 11787
ph: 631-265-1223
fax: 631-265-1602

Michael Compain, M.D.
Rhinebeck Health
108 Montgomery Street
Rhinebeck, NY 12572
ph: 845-876-7082
fax: 845-876-4615

Stephen Cowan, M.D.
14 Smith Avenue
Mt. Kisco, NY 10549
ph: 914-864-1976
fax: 914-864-1967

Paul Cutler, M.D.
652 Elmwood Avenue
Niagara Falls, NY 14301
ph: 716-284-5140

Joseph A. Debe, D.C., D.A.C.B.N.
38 Great Neck Road
Great Neck, NY 11021
ph: 516-829-1515
fax: 516-829-8578

Joseph A. Debe, D.C., D.A.C.B.N.
3174 Middle Country Road
Lake Grove, NY 11755
ph: 631-737-3660
fax: 631-737-3696

Moshe Dekel, M.D.
166 Elaine Drive
Oceanside, NY 11572
ph: 516-817-1770
fax: 516-992-5106

Michael Elice, M.D.
77 Froehlich Farms Boulevard
Woodbury, NY 11797
ph: 516-921-3456
fax: 516-364-1844

Giuseppina B. Feingold, M.D.
410 Route 6
Mahopac, NY 10541
ph: 845-208-3624
fax: 845-208-3626

Allan Goldblatt, P.A.-C.
77 Froehlich Farm Boulevard
Woodbury, NY 11797
ph: 516-921-3456
fax: 516-364-1844

Nancy Guberti, M.S.
Holistic Learning Center
571 A. White Plains Road
Eastchester, NY 10709
ph: 914-725-6801 or 793-9100
fax: 914-722-6043 or 793-3988

Michael A. Gruttadauria, D.C., D.A.C.A.N.
100 Manetto Hill Road,
Suite 106
Plainview, NY 11803
ph: 516-470-9525
fax: 516-470-9524

Christina Hift, M.D.
985 Fifth Avenue
New York, NY 10021
ph: 212-988-9011
fax: 212-861-0838

Raphael Kellman, M.D.
860 Fifth Avenue
New York, NY 10021
ph: 646-432-5552

Jeffrey C. Kopelson, M.D.
2 Executive Boulevard,
Suite 202
Suffern, NY 10901
ph: 845-368-4700
fax: 845-368-4727

Mitchell Kurk, M.D.
Lawrence Family Medical Practice,
P.C.
310 Broadway
Lawrence, NY 11559
ph: 516-239-5540
fax: 516-371-2919

Lawrence Palevsky, M.D.
220 Fort Salonga Road, Route 25A,
Suite 101
Northport, NY 11768
ph: 631-262-8505
fax: 631-754-2909

Kalpana Patel, M.D.
65 Wehrle Drive
Buffalo, NY 14225
ph: 716-837-1329
fax: 716-833-2244

Steven Rosman, Ph.D.
34 Lewis Lane
Port Washington, NY 11050
ph: 516-608-2806
fax: 516-608-6877

Richard Seibert, D.C.
1991 Merrick Avenue
Merrick, NY 11566
ph: 516-867-8585
fax: 516-867-1505

Alan Sherr, D.C.
220 Ft. Salonga Road
Northport, NY 11768
ph: 631-262-8505
fax: 631-754-2909

Morton Teich, M.D.
930 Park Avenue
New York, NY 10028
ph: 212-988-1821
fax: 212-288-9289

North Carolina

James Biddle, M.D.
Asheville Integrative Medicine
832 Hendersonville Road
Asheville, NC 28803
ph: 828-252-5545
fax: 828-281-3055

Anne Hines, M.D.
401 Northgate Park Drive
Winston-Salem, NC 27106
ph: 336-896-0954
fax: 336-714-1478

Nancy O'Hara, M.D.
7022 Sardis Road
Charlotte, NC 28270
ph: 203-834-2813
fax: 203-834-2831

John Pittman, M.D.
4505 Fair Meadow Lane,
Suite 111
Raleigh, NC 27607
ph: 919-571-4391
fax: 919-571-8968

Gail Szakacs, M.D.
7022 Sardis Road
Charlotte, NC 28270
ph: 203-834-2813
fax: 203-834-2831

Sharon Willingham, M.D.
Asheville Integrative Medicine
832 Hendersonville Road
Asheville, NC 28803
ph: 828-252-5545
fax: 828-281-3055

John Wilson, M.D.
Great Smokies Medical Center
1312 Patton Avenue
Asheville, NC 28806
ph: 828-252-9833
fax: 828-255-8118

Ohio

L. Terry Chappell, M.D.
122 Thurman Street
PO Box 248
Bluffton, OH 45817
ph: 419-358-4627
fax: 419-358-1855

Phillip DeMio, M.D.
320 Orchardview Avenue, Suite #2
Seven Hills, OH 44131
ph: 216-901-0441
fax: 216-901-0485

Phillip DeMio, M.D.
733-G Lakeview Plaza Boulevard
Worthington, OH 43085
ph: 614-436-2036
fax: 614-436-3169

Elizabeth A. Finley-Belgrad, M.D.
146 Forest Hill Road
Boardman, OH 44512
ph: 330-782-2438
fax: 330-782-2591

Robert M. Glad, M.D.
5764 Swan Creek Drive
Toledo, OH 43614
ph: 419-865-8455
fax: 419-479-6188

Cheryl Leuthaeuser, D.O.
Integrative WellCare
4003 Broadview Road
Richfield, OH 44286
ph: 330-659-2320
fax: 866-517-8990

Derrick Lonsdale, M.D.
24700 Center Ridge Road
Westlake, OH 44145
ph: 440-835-0104
fax: 440-871-1404

Deborah Nash, M.D., A.A.F.P.
423 W. Main Street
Tipp City, OH 45371
ph: 937-667-2222
fax: 937-667-5321

Maureen Pelletier, M.D.
5400 Kennedy Avenue
Cincinnati, OH 45213
ph: 513-924-5300
fax: 866-576-3554

Giovanna Vinci-Khoury, M.D.
Proposals for Healing
8790 E. Market Street, Suite 300
Warren, OH 44484
ph: 330-841-1189
fax: 330-841-7611

Oklahoma

Gerald Wootan, D.O.
715 W. Main Street
Jenks, OK 74037
ph: 918-299-9447
fax: 918-299-5325

Oregon

Leigh Ann Chapman, N.D.
Integrative Family Medicine
1567 SE Tacoma Street
Portland, OR 97202
ph: 503-233-8113

Rob Dramov, N.D.
9735 SW Shady Lane #104
Tigard, OR 97223
ph: 503-639-6454
fax: 503-639-6584

Mary Frazel, N.D.
2025 SE Jefferson Street
Milwaukie, OR 97222
ph: 503-654-5433
fax: 503-654-5439

John Green, M.D.
The Evergreen Center
516 High Street
Oregon City, OR 97045
ph: 503-722-4270
fax: 503-722-4450

Julie Glass, N.D.
Integrative Chiropractic &
Wellness Spa
9955 SE Washington Street, Suite 320
12616 SE Stark Street
Portland, OR 97216
ph: 503-522-6356
fax: 503-253-0377

Glenn Ingram, Jr., N.D.
Verbascum Naturopathic Health
1516 S.E. 43rd Avenue
Portland, OR 97215
ph: 971-219-8381

Alan Kadish, N.M.D., N.D.
2612 E. Barnett Road
Medford, OR 97504
ph: 541-773-3191
fax: 541-779-5647

Jennifer Reid, N.D.
27530 SE Division Drive,
Building C
Gresham, OR 97030
ph: 503-492-9427
fax: 503-492-7958

Pennsylvania

Franne R. Berez, M.D., N.D.
5801 Beacon Street
Pittsburgh, PA 15217
ph: 412-422-5433
fax: 412-422-1935

Philip L. Bonnet, M.D.
1086 Taylorsville Road
Washington Crossing, PA 18977
ph: 215-321-8321
fax: 215-321-9837

Leander Ellis, M.D.
2746 Belmont Avenue
Philadelphia, PA 18131
ph: 215-477-6444

Harold Grams, D.C.
326 Main Street
Red Hill, PA 18076
ph: 866-952-5483
fax: 215-679-6467

Denise Kelley, M.D.
Woodlands Healing Research Center
5724 Clymer Road
Quakertown, PA 18951
ph: 215-536-1890
fax: 215-529-9034

Roy Kerry, M.D.
17 Sixth Avenue
Greenville, PA 16125
ph: 724-588-2600
fax: 724-588-6427

Larry Miller, D.O.
2031 North Broad Street, Suite 121
Lansdale, PA 19446
ph: 215-412-4910
fax: 215-412-4911

Peter Prociuk, M.D.
322 North High Street
West Chester, PA 19380
ph: 610-701-5702
fax: 610-701-4225

Robert H. Schmidt, D.O.
Woodlands Healing Research Center
5724 Clymer Road
Quakertown, PA 18951
ph: 215-536-1890
fax: 215-529-9034

Puerto Rico

Yolanda Gonzalez-Roman, D.M.D.
PO Box 9058
San Juan, PR 00908
ph: 787-723-7844

Ada Ortiz Santiago, M.D.
Calle 1 D21 Altos de la Fuente
Caguas, PR 00727
ph: 787-743-2115
fax: 787-743-2115

Carmen Suarez, M.D.
31-43 Main Avenue
Santa Rosa, PR 00966
ph: 787-798-1300
fax: 787-740-0417

Rhode Island

Cathy Picard, N.D.
250 Eddie Dowling
Highway Unit 4
North Smithfield, RI 02896
ph: 401-597-0477
fax: 401-597-0959

South Carolina

Timothy J. Callaghan, M.D., D.C.
7510 Northforest Drive
North Charleston, SC 29420
ph: 843-572-1600
fax: 843-572-1795

Allan Lieberman, M.D.
7510 N. Forest Drive
N. Charleston, SC 29420
ph: 843-572-1600
fax: 843-572-1795

Tennessee

Paige E. Adams, M.S.N.
The Center for Proactive Medicine
1028 B 18th Avenue South
Nashville, TN 37212
ph: 615-331-1973
fax: 888-364-3905

Michael Bernui, D.O.
353 New Shackle Island Road, Suite 207A
Hendersonville, TN 37075
ph: 615-338-0123 / 888-833-0123
fax: 615-338-0553

Daniel B. Kalb, M.D., M.P.H.,
F.A.A.F.P.
Cool Springs Family Medicine
4091 Mallory Lane, Suite 118
Franklin, TN 37067
ph: 615-791-9784
fax: 615-791-9785

Texas

Kelly M. Barnhill, C.N.
Thoughtful House Center for
Children
3001 Bee Cave Road, Suite 120
Austin, TX 78746
ph: 512-732-8400
fax: 512-732-8353

Jeff D. Cunningham, D.C.
121 Hall Professional Circle, Suite A
Kyle, TX 78640
ph: 512-535-2922
fax: 512-853-9371

Lawrence Ginsberg, M.D.
17115 Red Oak Drive, #109
Houston, TX 77090
ph: 281-893-4111
fax: 281-893-8082

Bryan Jepson, M.D.
Thoughtful House Center for
Children
3001 Bee Cave Road, Suite 301
Austin, TX 78746
ph: 512-439-3800
fax: 512-439-3801

Alfred R. Johnson, D.O.
101 S. Coit Road, Suite 317
Richardson, TX 75080
ph: 972-479-0400
fax: 972-479-9435

Constantine Kotsanis, M.D.
2020 W. State Highway 114, Suite 260
Grapevine, TX 76051
ph: 817-481-6342
fax: 817-442-4848

Abby Kurth, M.P.H., M.S.
19141 Stone Oak Parkway #504
San Antonio, TX 78258
ph: 210-392-5500
fax: 210-495-3664

Frank Morales, M.D.
2805 Hackberry Lane
Brownsville, TX 78521
ph: 956-592-5584
fax: 956-544-4439

Carmen N. Otero-Arroyo, M.D.
Alamo City Center for Autism
1202 E. Sonterra Boulevard #302
San Antonio, TX 78258
ph: 210-572-0121
fax: 210-493-7050

Robert R. Somerville, M.D.
720 N. 77 Sunshine Strip
Harlingen, TX 78550
ph: 956-428-0757
fax: 956-428-8560

Arturo M. Volpe, D.C.
1714 Sunset Boulevard
Houston, TX 77005
ph: 713-529-5669
fax: 713-529-5590

Utah

Joseph Humpherys, N.M.D.
8537 S. Redwood Road, Unit B
West Jordan, UT 84088
ph: 801-565-3755
fax: 801-565-7171

David Voss, D.O.
Children's Biomedical Clinic
of Utah (CBC)
1675 N. Freedom Boulevard, #11E
Provo, UT 84604
ph: 801-373-8500
fax: 801-373-3426

Virginia

Margaret Gennaro, M.D.
10560 Main Street, Suite Ph-1
(6th Floor)
Fairfax, VA 22030
ph: 703-865-5692
fax: 703-865-5693

Warren Levin, M.D.
407 Church Street N.E., Suite E
Vienna, VA 22124
ph: 703-255-0313
fax: 703-255-0316

Eric Madren, M.D.
Princess Anne Medical Associates
1925 Glenn Mitchell Drive, Suite 100
Virginia Beach, VA 23456
ph: 757-689-8430
fax: 757-689-8435

Joseph Marcil, D.C.
Sports Med @ Gold's Gym
3809 Princess Anne Road
Virginia Beach, VA 23456
ph: 757-471-2800
fax: 757-471-4464

Mary Megson, M.D.
Pediatric & Adolesc. Ability Center
7229 Forest Avenue, Suite 211
Richmond, VA 23226
ph: 804-673-9128
fax: 804-673-9195

Eric N. Rydland, M.D., D.A.B.P.
1921 Commonwealth Drive
Charlottesville, VA 22901
ph: 434-984-5437
fax: 434-984-5439

Washington

Julie Anderson, A.R.N.P.
4757 36th Avenue South
Seattle, WA 98118
ph: 206-760-9266
fax: 206-760-9807

Leslie Charles, N.D.
6659 Kimball Drive, Suite C306
Gig Harbor, WA 98335
ph: 253-851-7550
fax: 253-851-7598

Hatha Gbedawo, N.D.
Vital Kids Medicine
1421 NW 70th Street
Seattle, WA 98117
ph: 206-782-1337
fax: 206-297-6118

Ralph Golan, M.D.
7522 20th Avenue NE
Seattle, WA 98115
ph: 206-524-8966
fax: 206-524-8951

Irfan Qureshi, N.D.
Pacific Highway Natural Medicine
15245 International Boulevard, Suite 210
Seatac, WA 98188
ph: 206-923-7600
fax: 206-923-7601

Philip Ranheim, M.D.
9407 4th Street NE
Lake Stevens, WA 98258
ph: 425-334-1773
fax: 425-334-5975

Rachel A. Robertson, N.D.
1145 Bethel Avenue
Port Orchard, WA 98366
ph: 360-876-5000
fax: 360-876-3389

Deborah Skalabrin, M.S.W.
701 W. 7th Avenue, Suite 15
Marycliff Hall
Spokane, WA 99204
ph: 509-448-1506

Stephen Smith, M.D.
Northwest Healthcare and Wellness
Center, PLLC
1901 George Washington Way,
Suite E
Richland, WA 99354
ph: 509-943-2101
fax: 509-943-2149

Mark Steinberg, N.D.
1313 E. Maple Street, #102
Bellingham, WA 98225
ph: 360-738-3230
fax: 360-738-4955

Michael Whitney, N.M.D., D.C.
North Spokane Natural Medical
Center
403 West Hastings Road
Spokane, WA 99218
ph: 509-465-5767
fax: 509-465-3570

West Virginia

Geeta Jayaram, M.D.
4403 44th Street
Charleston, WV 25304
ph: 304-925-4726
fax: 304-925-4869

Wisconsin

Gregory Brown, M.D.
ARCH Center
9612 S. Franklin Drive
Franklin, WI 53132
ph: 414-855-0240
fax: 414-855-0243

Gregg Hintz, Psy.D.
Therapeutic Pathways, SC
5219 88th Avenue
Kenosha, WI 53144
ph: 262-925-0425
fax: 262-653-0853

Norm Schwartz, M.D.
10602 N. Point Washington Road,
Suite 101
Milwaukee, WI 53092
ph: 262-240-0133
fax: 262-240-0194

Glenn Toth, M.D.
403 N. Grand Avenue
Waukesha, WI 53186
ph: 262-547-3055
fax: 262-547-2129

The author will donate a portion of her proceeds from this book to Generation Rescue. Families should not go without treatment. Generation Rescue will support families in need of care and fund research that will further science to help recover even more children with autism.

If you would like to donate to Generation Rescue, go to generationrescue.org.

Acknowledgments

Special thanks to:

Brian Tart, Trena Keating, Erika Imranyi, Jennifer Rudolph Walsh, Erwin More, and everyone at Dutton. I know our future together will only help heal the world even more. Thank you for believing in me.

ABOUT THE AUTHOR

Jenny McCarthy is the *New York Times* best-selling author of *Belly Laughs: The Naked Truth About Pregnancy and Childbirth; Baby Laughs: The Naked Truth About the First Year of Mommyhood; Life Laughs: The Naked Truth About Motherhood, Marriage, and Moving On,* and *Louder Than Words: A Mother's Journey in Healing Autism.* She lives in Los Angeles with her son, Evan, and Jim Carrey.